RECLAIMED

THIS CATHOLIC FAITH IS MINE!

Gregory Erich Phillips

"If any of you suffers as a Christian, do not consider it a disgrace, but glorify God because you bear this name. - I Peter 4:16

LIMA CONCORDIA

Published by Lima Concordia, Seattle, Washington.

ISBN-13: 978-0692025130
ISBN-10: 692025138

Cover photograph by Todd Gardiner.
Book design and typesetting by Spoddid™.
The text type was set in Adobe Garamond fonts.

Printed in the United States of America.
www.gregoryerichphillips.com

CONTENTS

PART I: THE POSITION OF TODAY'S CHRISTIAN

PART II: AN ACCOUNTABLE COMMUNITY

PART III: THE CHURCH IN THE MODERN WORLD

PART I:
THE POSITION OF TODAY'S CHRISTIAN

One: A Loving Challenge

"The message of the cross is foolishness… Since the world did not know God through wisdom, God decided, through the foolishness of our proclamation, to save those who believe. For God's foolishness is wiser than human wisdom, and God's weakness is stronger than human strength." - I Corinthians 1:18, 21, 25

"Aren't you a little ashamed to call yourself a Catholic these days?"

I cannot say the question surprised me, but it stung coming from such a close friend.

"It's one thing to believe all that stuff," she continued, "but how can you associate yourself with a backwards and corrupt organization like the Catholic Church, particularly the Vatican?"

My answer came quicker than I would have imagined.

"Actually, I am proud to be Catholic," I asserted. "And I am honored to consider the Pope my spiritual guide."

My friend walked away, confounded. To tell the truth, I was as surprised by what I had said as she was.

In the days and weeks that followed, I found myself reflecting more deeply on my answer than on her question. I realized that I had allowed myself to push my faith into the background of my life. When confronted, however, I was proud to call myself

Catholic. I look back with gratitude on that exchange as a pivotal moment in my development as a young Catholic man. It prompted me to reevaluate what my faith means in this day and age, amidst crises, scandals, and immersed in a world that does not want to hear the Gospel of Christ.

Today's Catholics find themselves in a challenging position. The culture in which we live, and the opinion of our peers, is at best ambivalent and at worst downright hostile toward a life of faith. At one time a strong Christian was admired, even by those who did not believe. Now that same Christian is often ridiculed. Many people view those who still subscribe to religion as old-fashioned—perhaps strangely admirable, yet unenlightened to the knowledge of the times, a full understanding of which would surely cause any modern-thinking man or woman to reject the mythic traditions of the past.

The last thing anyone wants to hear is our message—the word of truth we bear. Even those who may respect our decision to embrace faith remind us that, though our choice of religion is valid, their choice to reject faith is equally valid. What we consider true for us may not be true for them.

Hostility is easier to address than ambivalence. When Catholicism comes under wrongful accusation, I have no difficulty standing firm in defending it. But when I am told that another has found their own path—that they believe truth to be relative to each individual and deny me the opportunity to share the love that lies at the root of my own beliefs, what can I say? Though cased in words of peace and a false ecumenism, the message is clear: "I am not interested in your religion. Don't preach at me."

THE TRUE MEANING OF CHRISTIANITY

Part of this is our fault. Over the years, we have forgotten that the Christian message is truly "Good News!" There is joy in walking with Christ. We are renewed every day in his love. Unfortunately, Catholicism has often presented itself as a dogmatic rulebook. In actual fact, nothing could be further from the truth.

Ours is a religion of love—nothing else. God created us because of love, made the world beautiful because of love, came to meet us in our own human form, lived our life and died our death, all because of love. As Christians, we meet the world with a gift of love for every human being. If this remarkable truth did not underlie Christianity, there would be little motivation to follow its rules. The urgent message we bring to the world is that true and perfect love can be realized. The dogma—the so-called "law"— only has meaning within the context of wondrous love.

Unfortunately, we Christians have spent the greater part of our history burying our heads in dogma rather than proclaiming the reason for it. This, coupled with our failure to abide by our own rules, has caused the world to form opinions and judgments about us. They assume Catholics are intolerant, judgmental, and sexist. The world would like to see Catholicism fade away as a relic of a bygone age. The modern world takes for granted that it has us in retreat. It assumes that within another generation or two, our Catholicism will drift into memory, relegated to museums and history books. Many Catholics, though still strong in their own faith, have obliged the world's new creed of individualism. They no longer seek to make their faith and hope known to those around them.

The temptation is to meet this challenging environment with defeatism, antagonism or self-righteousness. But fighting fire with fire is not the Christian way. Rather, why not face such challenges with confidence and hope, a calm assurance of the truth and a humble pride in living for God?

Jesus never said that following him would be easy. He told us we would be ridiculed for our faith. Should we be surprised now that his words are coming true in our own time, and in our own personal lives? Why not reorient these negative thoughts so we can welcome the challenges of our time? As Christians, we have a hope stronger than anything the world can muster against us. So continue to proclaim the Good News, however little the world may want to hear it. The world still desperately needs the Good News.

We are the bearers of God's love. For this we should be both joyful and proud. The work is not easy, and we are admittedly flawed bearers of the Gospel. But this is the task for which God has made us *Lumen Gentium*—the Light of the World. If we do not take up the challenge, who will?

It is imperative that Christians comprehend just how loving our God is. Unless we understand the depth and nature of God's love, we will not be able to summon the inspiration to bring that love to others, nor will our hearts glow with the joyful honor of naming ourselves among his followers.

MY PURPOSE IN WRITING THIS BOOK

This book is meant to serve as an encouragement to modern Catholics, especially young Catholics, who face these challenges in their daily lives. I write as one of you, and I write this as a challenge to myself as much as to anyone. I am not a priest, nor do I hail from university halls. Rather, I write as a young professional in a bustling and secular American city. I experience pressure against my Catholicism every day. I am continually confronted by those who, like Paul, point out the "foolishness of following Christ." (I Cor. 1:18) I am a voice neither for Orthodoxy nor Progressivism within the Church. Rather, I speak from the belief that our challenges go beyond such political and doctrinal perspectives and must be addressed at a deeper level than the "hot-button" issues of the day.

Throughout my young adulthood, I have experienced the natural ebb and flow of spiritual fervor. My faith has been tested, not only from without, but from within. It has been a struggle at times to maintain my Christianity against the forces trying to tug me away. I face almost daily challenges from peers who are not only non-Christian, but *anti*-Catholic. Through the darkest of such personal doubts, I questioned some of the very fundamentals of our religion.

I, too, at times have been confounded by the image that the Vatican, and many within the ranks of the clergy, have presented to the world—an image inconsistent with one of loving and shepherding leadership. What a breath of fresh air Francis's young papacy has been toward establishing a truly pastoral leadership model.

It was through a series of personal challenges from people close to me, such as the one I described earlier, that I felt God inject me with new confidence in my faith. It is that confidence, the same confidence the Holy Spirit instilled in the disciples at Pentecost, which I wish to share with you. On that day, the disciples went pouring into the streets, joyful and consumed with pride to follow Christ. May we experience Pentecost anew in our time, with equal joy and equal pride.

I pray this book will prove valuable to young Catholics like me who find themselves being pulled this way and that by multiple religious and secular factions. I pray it will likewise speak to all Catholics hungry to transcend the contentious issues of our day and return to the basic truths of Christianity, the sublimity of faith, and the breathtaking example, personified in the world two thousand years ago, of the incarnate God we follow.

Lord God, make me a vessel of your love for those you have put in my life. Help me to shine as a light into a world filled with darkness and division. Let my joy in following you be visible to the world around me.

MAKE IT MINE

APPLYING THE LESSONS FROM THIS CHAPTER IN MY LIFE:

➤ Do I sometimes feel embarrassed to tell people I'm Catholic? Why?

➤ Spend some thoughtful and prayerful moments thinking about why you are a Catholic. If you have stopped practicing, what pushed you away?

➤ Look for some ways to visibly demonstrate your spiritual beliefs (whatever they may be) in your daily life.

Two: A New Pentecost

"And the doors of the house where the disciples had met were locked for fear. Jesus came and stood among them and said… 'Peace be with you. As the Father has sent me, so I send you.' When he had said this, he breathed on them and said, 'Receive the Holy Spirit.'" - John 20:19, 22

In the early days of Christendom, fear ruled the disciples' hearts. The earliest copies of Mark's gospel end with the words, "they were afraid."

Jesus was gone. Their enemies had won. If they took their Christian message to the streets, the best they could hope for was to be laughed at for following a dead man. At worst, they would share his execution. Lacking the courage to live out their faith in a hostile world, they locked themselves in an upper room.

The position of today's Catholics is similar. In a sense, we are back in that upper room, locked away in the safety of our community, timid to be vocal about our faith in a hostile world.

It is hardly a secret that the cultural pressure of the world is vehemently opposed to Christian principles. The supposed sages of knowledge claim to have moved beyond the ideas of religion. Jesus, our Lord and leader, is acknowledged as a great teacher of morality, but the idea of his being God incarnate is dismissed as an unenlightened myth of ancient folklore. I find that whenever I attempt to offer intelligent insight, be it on culture, science, or philosophy, as soon as my hearer realizes that my perspective and world view is Christian, my word is dismissed. A Christian outlook on the world is no longer considered valid by society or academia.

CHRISTIANITY'S PURPOSE IN THE WORLD

The response from many is to retreat into the cocoon of our churches and faith communities, where we can worship without fear of ridicule. This, however, defeats the purpose of Christianity. Not for a moment discounting the value of personal and communal worship, the true nature of Christianity is not an inward, but an outward religion. God calls us to meet the world as we encounter it, bringing the light of Christ to the world through love, compassion, peace, and justice.

We are also called to share our hope, for which the world desperately thirsts.

The Second Vatican Council admonished all Christians not to "hide their hope in the depths of their hearts, but rather express it through the structure of their secular lives in continual conversion." An honest Christian cannot ignore the call to be a light to the world. "No one after lighting a lamp puts it under the bushel basket, but on the lamp-stand, and it gives light to all the house. In the same way, let your light shine before others, so that they may see your good works and give glory to your Father in heaven." (Matt. 5:15-16) Christianity demands participation in the world.

Pope Emeritus Benedict XVI asked: "How could the idea have developed that Jesus' message is… aimed only at each person singly? How did we arrive at this interpretation of the 'salvation of the soul' as a flight from responsibility for the whole, and how did we come to conceive the Christian project as a selfish search for salvation which rejects the idea of serving others?" My sense is that the timidity many of us feel is rooted in fear—fear of being sneered at or rejected by our peers, fear of being ignored, and yes, even fear of being wrong.

Yet we are in good company. The founders of Christianity were the same disciples who ran away when Jesus was arrested, denied knowing him at his trial, and then locked themselves away in a hidden room after he was gone.

Then something changed.

What jolted these men out of their timidity, making them so bold of faith that most were eventually executed for testifying to the Christ they had once abandoned?

In the time shortly after Jesus' ascension, his disciples did not understand his message or their mission. Even after his death and resurrection, they still expected him to free Israel from Rome and establish an earthly kingdom. (Acts 1:6) Not until Pentecost did they begin to realize what he had been trying to tell them all along—that his kingdom was not of this world. (John 18:36) This was not easy for them to come to terms with.

But something remarkable happened at Pentecost. Suddenly, the disciples were transformed. From a fearful gathering huddled in a locked room, they poured into the streets and proclaimed the Gospel of Christ with intense fervor. They were filled with such confidence that they literally could not be shut up. Strengthened with this confidence, they carried Christianity to the far corners of the world. It cost most of them their lives.

We are now back in that upper room, not fearing for our lives, but fearing ridicule, loss, and shame. But the world needs us, just as it needed Jesus' first disciples. It is a selfish Christianity that remains behind the safety of locked doors. It is not true Christianity at all.

A NEW CALLING FOR OUR TIME

Our calling today differs from what it was for Peter, John, and the rest of the early apostles. We live in a world that has already heard the message of Jesus, and has even partially accepted it. Our culture has not entirely rejected Christ's Gospel, but it has only incorporated those elements of the message it finds convenient. If we were to hit the streets and preach Christ's message at the top of our lungs as the disciples did, we would be sneered at in the same way and thought to be "filled with new wine." (Acts 2:13) Our task is different. When we leave our churches for the streets, it should be with a gospel of visible love and exampled charity. Only thus will we prove the true meaning of Christianity.

Ours is not a creed of words and reflection, but a creed of action and participation.

St. Francis of Assisi said to preach the gospel at all times, and when necessary to use words. He understood that the truest and most effective evangelism does not require the spoken word at all.

Surrounded by our society's secular environment, and not grasping this balance, Christians are tempted by two extremes. Some don't use *enough* words, choosing to keep their faith hidden behind the comfortable walls of their churches. Others use *too many* words in combating the secular pressure coming at us from every angle. By relying exclusively on words, we may do more harm than good to our message. Words are powerful and must be chosen with care. Too much talk actually makes the world *less* receptive to the Gospel.

The world needs our love and compassion more than it needs what we have to say. Even the best chosen words fall short alongside what can be accomplished through actions and behavior—by life *lived*. It is in the preaching of deeds that those around us will take notice.

St. James tells us, "*If a brother or sister is naked and lacks daily food, and one of you says to them, 'Go in peace,' and yet you do not supply their bodily needs, what is the good of that?*" (James 2:15, 16) James reminds us that faith is shared *first* through acts of goodness. Only then, *after* a foundation of love has been laid, are we in a position to testify to the truth which inspired our deeds.

Christianity comes to the world as an *active* religion, one which demands not our words, but our works of love in the world.

Lord God, give me the courage not to be a mere Upper Room Christian. Fill me with the inspiration of a new Pentecost, strengthened by the Holy Spirit. Make me proud to profess, through my actions, the hope the world so desperately needs.

MAKE IT MINE!

APPLYING THE LESSONS FROM THIS CHAPTER IN MY LIFE:

➤ Am I an "Upper Room Christian?" Is my religion something private, or is it an active and visible part of my life?

➤ Where are your "upper rooms?" Where do you go (either physically or emotionally) to feel safe about your religion? In so doing, are you selling the Christian message short?

➤ Look for opportunities in your daily life to bring the spirit of Pentecost "into the streets." Preach the gospel with deeds rather than words.

Three: They Will Know We Are Christians By Our Love

"I give you a new commandment, that you love one another. Just as I have loved you, you also should love one another. By this everyone will know that you are my disciples, if you have love for one another." - John 13:34-35

If the world were asked to describe Christianity with a single word, what would it be?

The possibilities sting my ears. It saddens me to hear Christianity described as intolerant, outdated, hypocritical, sexist, and so many other unflattering adjectives. Every day I see books and news articles not only scoffing at Christianity, but *blaming* it, and Catholicism in particular, for many of society's ills. A co-worker recently told me, in no uncertain terms, that she believed *all* the injustice in the world had been caused by religion having poisoned human thought.

While this should not surprise me—we were never promised the esteem of the world—it still breaks my heart. What a terrible indictment against us!

A SIMPLE FOUNDATION FOR EVERYTHING—LOVE

How different is the truth upon which our faith was founded.

If a single word were used to describe Christianity, that word should be *love*.

15

Why should I choose to follow the tenets of Christianity rather than the easier paths of freedom and ambivalence? Why have I united myself to a difficult creed, taken on the scorn of my peers, and embarked on a path which promises a cross?

I have chosen Christianity, quite simply, because it promises love. Everything within Christianity reduces to love.

The reward of God's love is so great that we willingly follow the way of the cross in hope of his everlasting embrace. By opening our hearts in love toward our neighbors, we feel that divine embrace even now. This hope drives us on the difficult journey called Christianity, even throughout all its trials.

Every observation I make of our world speaks of unbounded love. When I consider the beauty of the earth, the intricate operations of nature and the human body, *everything* speaks of the goodness of God's gifts to his creation. God could perhaps have made a world that is not wonderful, but he did make it wonderful because he loves us: because he loves *me*, loves *you*, loves each of us individually and uniquely.

Love, at its core, is an expression of giving. It defines a communion between lover and beloved. In love, one pours oneself into another. Love is never selfish. It hoards nothing unto itself, but only desires to *give*. True love asks nothing in return for this outpouring. Its very nature is to give.

What else can explain the beauty and wonder of creation and its remarkable energy of life? Apart from love, there is no overarching meaning or sense to creation. It begins to appear utterly nonsensical. No foundational cause other than love can explain why anything *good* should exist at all.

LOVE DEFINES BOTH GOD'S ESSENCE AND OUR OWN

John the Evangelist makes a startling declaration. He goes beyond saying that God loves us. He reveals that God *is* love. (I John 4:16) Love is who he is. No wonder everything in God's creation shouts of love. This seems too good to be true, but it is this revelation and promise that inspires us to follow the Christian faith. The God we love and serve is love itself.

Can God really be love itself? Can he be *that* good?

One is almost tempted to discard John's statement simply because it points toward *too* great a hope. It takes daring to believe such a beautiful promise. Indeed, to face assault on Christianity from every side, it actually takes *courage* to stand firm in the belief that God is love.

We cannot allow the pressures of our culture against faith to rob us of so magnificent a wonder. It is upon this foundational truth that Christianity is built. John's high revelation points toward the full extent of God's goodness. Everything beautiful, everything good, and everything true is a free gift of love to us. God showers us with love. All he asks in return is that we love others as he has loved us. (John 13:34)

Am I naïve for believing something so wonderful? That is often the response to Christian hope. I would rather say that this conviction makes me a believer in what the universe shouts as *true,* no matter how difficult it may be to see it with temporal eyes.

Not only does love describe who God is. It also describes who we are.

Love is the greatest desire of the human heart. Love is so important to us that we value it more than life itself. Love is the personal contact with others that validates our human experience. What greater miracle of life can exist than two hearts sharing a loving bond? That we are created in God's image is a truth that binds creator and created in a unity of mutual love. Love seals the eternal compact between us and God and between ourselves and others of our kind.

Yet human love frequently fails to satisfy. The parent or lover who showers endless love on child or beloved often receives rejection in return. Love is both our greatest joy and our greatest source of pain.

Our experience with love, both in the joy of reciprocation and in the despair of rejection, mirrors God's own. God created us because he is love. Yet love is lonely until it finds, and is able to *actively* love, its beloved. God *needed* to create because his very nature is to create and love—we are both child and beloved of God. Since God is love, he desires community in which love can be expanded. We are the benefactors of the parental instinct in God's heart—a great desire to expand his love.

God bestows upon us limitless generosity and patience. Our ungratefulness never hinders him. Each and every one of us, individually, is the beloved of God himself. God gave me not only my life, but all the gifts of the world as a sign of his love. Should I consider it an obligation to return God's love? I would hope that my response to his love reaches far beyond that. Rather, it is a *joy* to reciprocate such a love as this!

Through the observation of God's gifts to me and to all of humanity, it naturally follows for me to understand the importance of giving likewise to those around me. To do so is simply following God's example. Charity and compassion thus become vital elements of Christian love. I have done nothing to deserve the gifts God has given me. How can I be possessive of those gifts and not share them with others? I reciprocate God's love by extending my own love toward those with whom I share his gift of life.

God's gifts do not function by the laws of human economy. When we give of what God has given us, we suffer no shortage. There is no limit to the abundance of God's giving. The more we give, the more God continues to bless us from his abundance.

JESUS' LOVE IS SHOCKINGLY UNIQUE

Jesus gave us our example. He loved every man, every woman and every child he encountered without expecting reciprocation. He showed the path to true love—giving without expecting anything in return. Only by loving with true unselfishness can we find contentment and open ourselves to God's blessings.

Faith in Jesus' example is the reason to follow the Christian creed. I desire with all my heart to share in God's remarkable love. The reward of God's love is so wonderful that I am willing to endure whatever hardships may come as a result of my faith.

There is, however, another side to the love that is the foundational essence of the Christian faith. Not only is love the natural order of the universe, the natural outflowing of God's abundant nature, but, as God's children, we are also *commanded* to love. It is not a choice. God gives expecting nothing in return—except that we do the same. We must learn to be like him in making love the ruling power of our lives.

The love Jesus showed is different from anything the world had previously known. It is a completely selfless love. Søren Kierkegaard identified the Christian concept of *Thou Shalt Love* as something foreign to any prior notion of love. Until the *shalt* entered the equation, love was always changeable. "Only when it is a duty to love," Kierkegaard wrote, "only then is love everlastingly secure against every change; everlastingly emancipated in blessed independence, everlastingly happy, assured against despair." [1] The word, *shalt*, implies command, insistence, *must*. Only thus can love be utterly true.

Christian love, first an order, then a duty, becomes a liberation. We have been taught Christian love for so long that we forget how revolutionary it is. "Forget for a moment Christian love, and consider what you know about other forms of love. Recall what you read in the poets, what you yourself can discover, and then say whether it ever occurred to you to conceive this: *Thou shalt love!*"[2]

The world, tormented by false and changeable love, needs the comfort and stability of Christian love.

But if Christianity is a religion of love, how did it come to be seen as something so different? Rather than a religion of love, modern society perceives Christianity as intolerant and restrictive. The disconnect between religion and modern values will be explored in the next chapter, but that disconnect is only part of the problem. The rest of it is our fault. It is true that Christianity sets forth a creed and a set of laws for life. But creed and law do not define Christianity. The foundation, again, is love. Law emerges out of that love. The sad truth is that we have not visibly and selflessly *lived* the love that undergirds our creed.

---

[1] Søren Kierkegaard: *Works of Love*, Part 1, IIa

[2] ibid

CHRISTIAN LOVE MAY YET CHANGE THE WORLD

So much of each person's effort in life is motivated by the desire to find love. Even many common sins emerge from a perverted desire for love. If, in Christianity, the world could observe a fulfillment of the desire for love and witness the example of those who have found it, selfish and depraved goals would lose their luster. Humanity's greatest desire is love. The hearts of our time will only change if we appeal to this most basic need and offer a unique and distinctive love that satisfies it.

Christianity is pitted against the world in foundational ways. As Christian values struggle against today's culture of freedom, morality itself is at stake. In the world's eyes, *any* behavior can be excused by claiming it as an individual's "right." So-called *rights* have no barriers. Morality in any universal sense has ceased to be considered valid. The Christian counters such modernism with the virtues and codes by which God has commissioned us to live.

So often, however, we allow the world to lure us into a battle of ideas on its own terms. The discussion between Christian morality and the self-motivated "rights" of modernism degenerates into a struggle over political and social issues rather than the nature of truth itself. If instead, we could show the world the love which leads us to believe as we do, the evangelism of our values would carry far greater weight. The greatest victories are not won in courts and legislatures, but in the hearts of men and women.

Love is the reason we are Christians. The world *needs* to see this. The future effectiveness of our faith hinges upon this, and *only* this. There should be a discernible difference between every interaction with a

Christian versus an interaction with a non-Christian. They must know we are Christians by our love (John 13:35), by our compassion, by our charity. Then perhaps an increasingly non-Christian and spiritually ambivalent world may wonder why we believe what we do and be intrigued to learn more. The social and political activism of Christianity will only carry weight if the world recognizes its inherent love.

At present, the world views Christians as intolerant. While we rightly fight against injustice in our society, if we do so without love, we degenerate into one more political lobby. We have continually made this error. As a result the world perceives Christian views on social issues as dogmatic restrictions of freedom. If the world could understand the love that lies at the root of our views and doctrines, it would listen with greater receptivity. All God's commandments are founded in love and embraced by that love.[3] If we truly and visibly *lived* this truth, the world might be more attracted to the commandments.

In a society in which freedom and personal satisfaction entices the majority, it surprises people to learn that we choose instead to follow Christ. We *choose* not to be lured by false freedoms, but to live under the constraints of a chosen obedience.

The world looks at us with wonder and asks *why*.

Despite constant attempts to pry us away, we have chosen the harder path. The reason is simple: God's love satisfies as nothing else can. Even through suffering, the joyful companionship of Jesus is steadfast. We want to follow his commandments because they are embraced by love.

---

[3] St. Augustine of Hippo: *Enchiridion*, 121

The world has heard us trumpet the law. But love both precedes and fulfills the law.

Jesus is the proof of God's love. By becoming one of us, God shows that he is more than the omnipotent creator—the master and judge of the universe. He is also our friend, our companion, and sharer in our suffering. By laying aside the glory and power of heaven, emptying himself into the helpless embryo of an unborn baby, and then experiencing the joys and sorrows of life from the vulnerable perspective of humanity, God *proves* his love for us.

As Christians, we believe in a God who loves us so much that he would show us the way to salvation by example, not merely by law. This is the remarkable uniqueness of Christianity among all the creeds in the world.

THE HEART OF LOVE—SELFLESS GIVING

Life is hard.

We are all acquainted with suffering. Some suffer physically, others emotionally, while some suffer from afflictions brought upon themselves. But we have all suffered in some way. Humanity shares this. Yet suffering is nearly always tempered by softer influences. In God's redemptive economy, even suffering becomes infused with his love and contains the potential to draw us closer to him.

Because the world's quest for love is largely selfish, its misguided efforts to find love often cause even more suffering. Selfish love is not truly love at all; it usually produces more pain than joy. To be received with its full beauty and power, love must first be *given*—given unselfishly, without strings.

In our society of immediate gratification, the self*less*ness of true love is not intuitive. It is hardly any wonder the world fails to understand this basic component of love's function. This illuminates the cause for much of the world's misery. It also explains why the simple answer given by Christianity to the world's suffering so often falls on deaf ears.

Every individual I meet presents me with the opportunity to spread the love of Christ. I am called to love everyone with my whole heart, despite their faults, deformities, arrogance, or sin. I am called to commit my heart to true compassion for the suffering of those around me.

SUFFERING TRANSFORMED BY LOVE

Love is hardly an "answer" to the pervasive suffering all around us, but it is the balm that soothes and comforts the world's pain.

God pleads with us to respond to the world's suffering with acts of love. Out of the evil that has come into the world, he is eager to work good through us. We are the agents of God's good *into* the world's pain.

Seen in this higher and purposeful light, suffering takes on a truly salvific significance. [4] Such is the Christian's duty toward those wrapped in suffering. It is our opportunity to take part with God in bringing salvation's love to the world.

The greatest beauty we can find in the world will be discovered in the compassionate love we show to our brothers and sisters of humanity. In your own heart you have the answer to the world's suffering—love.

---

[4] Pope John Paul II: *Salvifici Doloris,* 30

You may not be able to ease the whole world's suffering, but you have the opportunity to ease *someone's* suffering. We all have many suffering *someones* at our doorsteps.

As Christians we *are* called to change the world, one loving encounter at a time.

If the world observes us living lives of love, compassion, and charity, it will wonder about the source of that commitment. When those around us see the truth of Christ's love as a living reality in the conduct of our daily affairs, they will be curious about our creed.

When I love, I am acting as the love of God toward others. When I receive love, it is God's love, working through others, coming into my life. *"God is love, and those who abide in love abide in God, and God abides in them."* (I John: 4:16). These words pinpoint the reason why I am a Christian.

Christianity gives us a daily renewal in God's love, experienced intimately through the love of one another. This is the great promise of God's kingdom.

Eternal life does not begin at death. Our eternal life has already begun! We experience it daily by sharing the love God has poured out on us and into us.

Lord God, let me approach the world with the motivation that some day when Christianity is described in one word, that word will be love.

MAKE IT MINE!

APPLYING THE LESSONS FROM THIS CHAPTER IN MY LIFE:

➤ Is my Christianity apparent in my attitude? Would a stranger, on meeting me, discern that there is something different about me?

➤ Think honestly about what single words the people in your life might use to describe you. If they are not flattering words, then focus and pray about how to change the perception people have of you.

➤ Look for opportunities in your daily life to demonstrate Christian love in specific and tangible ways. Make people wonder at you!

Four: The World's "Freedom-God"[5]

"Blessed are you when people revile you and persecute you and utter all kinds of evil against you on my account. Rejoice and be glad, for your reward is great in heaven." - Matthew 5:11-12

In calling Catholics to take pride in their religion, it would be imprudent for me not to acknowledge the shortcomings of the Catholic Church. Its failure, oftentimes, to "practice what it preaches" is the very reason a book like this is needed.

There can be no doubt that the Church has made dreadful mistakes throughout its history and continues making new ones today. The whole world is aware of these faults, we Catholics perhaps most keenly of all. That said, the focus of this book is elsewhere. This book is intended to challenge Catholics to take pride in what they believe and in the faith tradition which accompanies it. Pope Francis said he prefers a Church that is wounded due to its involvement with the world to one that keeps itself closed off.[6]

Significant to the present discussion is the effect the Church's scars have had on the faithful and what

---

[5] Much of the material from this chapter appeared in my article: *Stand Up and Follow Christ*, Social Justice Review, V. 98, 3-4, St. Louis

[6] Pope Francis: Letter to the Argentine Episcopal Conference, March 25, 2013

we have to do to win back the good opinion of the world. I have felt pangs of guilt and sadness every time I heard of a priest accused of abuse. I have been confused by seemingly divisive proclamations coming from the Vatican. Daily I fall prey to outright hostility toward Catholicism from my peers, even from my closest friends. It is hard to take pride in my faith when I am continually reminded of Catholicism's failings. In this environment it is difficult not to feel shy of speaking openly about my beliefs.

Counterintuitively, this hostility is not rooted in the Church's historic flaws, the misconduct of its priesthood, or the hypocrisy of its members. These only give the world its excuse. Our errors, both as a Church and individually, provide the world with ammunition to attack a creed it does not want to hear. But while our sins show that we cannot live up to the standards we preach, that is certainly no reason to stop preaching them. The world is antagonistic because Christianity declares a creed that clashes with modern values, specifically the modern idea of *freedom*. Christianity demands that I think first not of myself but of others—not a popular concept these days.

FREEDOM—THE DECEPTIVE GOD OF OUR AGE

The most valued moral of our age is *freedom*. The lust for so-called "freedom" has become so insatiable that we have ceased to understand what the word really means.

This all-encompassing desire for freedom rose out of the Enlightenment in the seventeenth century, and this individualist philosophy gradually began to dominate Western thought. Radical changes in society sprang from this new understanding of freedom.

Totalitarian governments and class-based societies became unacceptable. The revolutions of Europe and America showed how far people would go to attain freedom. The concept of democracy became the new model for society. We are accustomed to it now, but the expectation for the way a moral government should operate contrasts sharply today with how the world functioned only a few centuries ago.

Freedom, of course, is good, but freedom is not everything. Nor should we treat freedom as the ultimate virtue to be attained. Freedom can go too far. One need only look at the philosophy of Karl Marx, once hailed as the natural successor to Enlightenment thinking, to see how freedom can be corrupted. He envisioned "communist" society (in his ideal, one of complete equality) as capable of giving everyone personal freedom. The history of governmental communism since his time underscores the failure of his philosophy.

The reality is all too clear: One person's grasp for freedom often thwarts the freedom of another. When the poor and oppressed wage revolution against those whom they perceive have taken away their freedoms, their goal is often to abolish the freedom of those in power. Perhaps one may consider them justified in doing so, but usually they go too far. Prior to the French revolution in the 1790s, freedoms in that society were grossly skewed. The nobility had disproportionate freedom at the expense of the poor. The revolution, in fact, skewed it *worse* in the opposite direction. Those of the former nobility were deprived of the most basic freedom of all—life itself. The revolution as a cultural event may have succeeded, but it did not succeed in achieving equitable freedom. It simply gave disproportionate freedom to a select few—a new and different select few. It replaced one elite with another. The Bolshevik revolution a century and a quarter later in Russia had the same result.

Unfettered freedom cannot be had by everyone. Those who attempt to live in complete freedom consider themselves justified in ignoring laws they feel infringe upon their rights. In doing so, however, they flout the freedoms of others. Freedom always falls prey to the corruption of greed. A healthy society, therefore, must balance a multitude of desired "freedoms" among all its citizens.

FREEDOM REQUIRES LAW

Pope Benedict XVI wrote extensively on this dual dichotomy and impossibility, warning against placing too much value on the *idea* of freedom, while missing its deeper meaning. "The freedom of man is a shared freedom," he wrote as Cardinal Ratzinger. "[It is] freedom in a coexistence of other freedoms, which are mutually limiting and thus mutually supportive… If the freedom of man can only continue to exist within an ordered coexistence of freedoms, then this means that order—law—is, not the concept contrary to that of freedom, but its condition, indeed, a constitutive element of freedom itself. Law is not the obstacle to freedom; rather, it constitutes freedom." From these words comes the surprising, but ultimately logical, conclusion that "the absence of law is the absence of freedom."[7] True freedom actually *requires* law.

---

[7] Joseph Cardinal Ratzinger: *Freedom & Truth, Communio* 23

It is easy to see how law is necessary in society. The same principle also applies to morality. Societal law (justice) restricts only far enough to prevent one person from injuring another. Morality, however, reaches further, into the very depths of what constitutes our intrinsic humanity. Here the Christian places a restriction upon individual moral freedom no less than upon society at large. Justice is by no means the same thing as morality.

Modern culture balks at this point. Freedom has become modernism's god. Justice is still given credence, but moral absolutes are not valued because people do not want to be told what to do. Sinful and hurtful practices are justified under the banner of personal individuality. People claim as their "right" the freedom to do whatever makes them happy. Any moral code that attempts to limit an individual's freedom is considered intolerant.

The end result is that modern culture has convinced itself that truth and morality are relative and that every individual has the right to pick and choose what constitutes truth and morality for himself or herself. We, as a culture, have become so besotted with the idea of freedom that we have lost the wisdom to see the logical absurdity of this foundation stone of modernism. Scarce wonder that truth in our time has become a ship without a rudder.

Thus the former Pope emphasized that freedom must be linked to "a yardstick of truth." [8] Without *Absolute* Truth, and the law that accompanies it,

---

[8] ibid

individual freedoms cancel each other out. In the end, relativism ultimately results in a return to a primitive chaos wherein the strong believe they are free, yet their so-called freedom can only be had at the expense of the weak.

It is an undeniable truth that, within a society, no single individual's freedom can be separated from the freedom of the rest. This truth forms the basis for societal justice. Christianity goes a step further in offering a *moral* law with a goal of shared freedom of all, strong and weak, rich and poor. To modernism, Christianity's moral code may appear to be a limitation of freedom. But in fact, it provides the only true regulating compass capable of producing betterment for the human race as a whole.

Because the Catholic Church does not condone the wide and unlimited personal moral freedoms that progressivism clamors for, it is considered intolerant. Christianity makes a claim of truth. Whatever may be our faults, we will always insist on proclaiming *Truth*. This claim, in itself, is unacceptable to modern cultural relativism.

DOES CHRISTIANITY OFFER FREEDOM? YES AND NO

What does Christianity have to say about the freedom the world so craves?

The answer may surprise you. It is mute. Christianity offers no freedom, only humility. Jesus commands the slave to work diligently and respectfully for his master and the captive nation of Israel to submit to the rule of Rome. Such commands hardly reflect the *freedom-god* values of modern culture.

The Church is under tremendous pressure from the *culture of tolerance* in which we live and its *freedom-god*. The secular media, and even certain voices within the Church itself, insist that unless the Church spreads a wider umbrella of tolerance and acceptance, it will make itself an insignificant vestige of the past.

In actuality, the Church *does* accept everyone. But it does *not* accept actions or practices that go against its claim of truth. The only true threat of insignificance will arise when the Church bows to this pressure by relinquishing the moral code upon which it is based.

Today's culture of tolerance results in a treacherous tightrope which most Christians don't quite know how to navigate. Our ambient culture takes pride in its tolerance for *all* lifestyles, actions, and creeds. However, it has *no* tolerance for a creed which claims to be *true*. Because of its claim of *real,* not *relative,* truth, Christianity has become the primary target of scorn from the "politically correct" tolerance of modern culture.

The values of the culture which surrounds us make being a Christian very tricky these days. Much as a Christian may disagree with values or actions of another, judgmentalism and intolerance have never been Christian values! Our first and highest calling is to love all men and women, including those who are not walking according to Christianity's moral code. Nor are we in a position to reprimand their choices until they seek our council or the council of the Church.

The example of Jesus is always our guide in walking this tightrope. He repeatedly dined with both tax collectors and prostitutes. He welcomed them into his inner circle. Yet there is no doubt about his feelings toward the practices of financial cheating and adultery. In response to the former, he drove the money-changers from the temple in such dramatic fashion that it undoubtedly contributed to his death sentence. (Mark 11:15-18) As to adultery, he condemned it in stronger words than have ever been spoken either before or after (Matt. 5:28). Jesus gives no excuse for intolerance toward individuals, even though we *must* oppose certain behavior.

We believe that Jesus is the Son of God. We serve him through works of love and charity. If we bow to contemporary culture to the degree that we no longer make this claim, we will have lost the essence of Christianity. While we should be tolerant toward those of other lifestyles, even those who practice other religions, we *cannot* bow to the pressures of our culture to the point that we sacrifice the essence of Christian morality—the law which provides our shared freedom. Once we yield to this pressure and abandon our values, we will no longer have truth to offer to those who seek the Church as a haven of love.

The moral law of Christianity may be the cause of its rift with modernism, but it is precisely its rigorous morality that keeps the Church relevant.

HUMANITY'S SUPPOSED FREEDOM

The world views truth and freedom through the same lens. Neither is considered absolute.

The search for truth, long the universal objective of philosophy, has now been replaced by personal experience. There is no more Truth in the upper case—

Absolute Truth. What is called *truth* has become the mere relativism of varying personal experiences and opinions. It is essentially an *a posteriori* "perspective" on truth. Obviously, this perspective will differ for everyone. By definition, experience and opinion *must* be distinct for all. Thus, *Absolute Truth* is no longer sought. Today's philosophic academia tends not to even believe it exists.

This philosophic change of the last few centuries is rooted in the new valuation of freedom. The Age of Enlightenment taught of an individualistic freedom, which extended to the freedom of thought and ideas. This is how the idea arose that truth was relative— subject to the whim of each individual.

As culture (and the Church) was revolutionized in the 1960s, the morality of "freedom" became the model and rallying cry of a new generation. Popular culture no longer valued sacrifice and vocation, but rather individual freedom. As a result, the seminaries emptied. Many of the priests who remained fell into a pattern of abuse. Due to this changed cultural value set, the life of a priest over the last fifty years, particularly in America and Europe, has arguably been harder than at any other time in history. The Church has had a difficult time, and has made many false starts, in attempting to show itself valid to a culture with dramatically new norms.

In accepting all viewpoints as equally legitimate because every individual must have the "freedom" to think as he or she chooses, modern society has adopted a pluralism, based, in the words of Pope John Paul II, "upon the assumption that all positions are equally valid. This is one of today's most widespread symptoms of the lack of confidence in truth… All claims of truth have been reduced to mere opinion."[9] In such a cultural atmosphere, Christianity is considered intolerant even before it makes its claim of truth, simply because it *does* make a claim of truth.

What right have we, the world asks, to make a claim of truth at all?

How are we to reconcile the moral shortcomings of both Church leaders and the Church itself with our current scandals and our history of violence and persecution?

How dare we preach morality? Should we not hide away behind our church doors until we ourselves can get it right?

Yet it is our own failings that illustrate the veracity of the truth we offer. If we were not sinners, we would have no need of a savior. Does the fact that I am a sinner make me a hypocrite for condemning sin?

The continuation of Catholicism, even with all its egregious errors, is proof that God's grace continues to operate among sinful men and women—and even within a sinful Church.

This is a difficult time to be a Catholic. But it is now imperative not to slacken our moral values or our belief in Absolute Truth. The work of Christ is unending. Through love and charity, we continue his work. Only thus will we recover our reputation in the world.

THE POSITION OF TODAY'S CHRISTIAN
Where has all this left the modern Christian?

---

[9] Pope John Paul II: *Fides et Ratio*, 5

When I tell people I am Catholic, they seem to find it quaint. But it is clear that a whole range of assumptions and judgments immediately fall into place in their minds. They do not exactly snicker to my face, but their eyes inwardly roll. They assume that I find my religion (it is always "religion," not "reality," in their view) fulfilling for myself, but do not interpret my stand as having anything to say about truth which might impact them. They have no interest in hearing about the hope and love which constitute my faith. It is all relative; these have no bearing on their lives. They could not care less. Uppercase *Truth* is a non-entity in their world. It simply does not exist.

As Christians, we are left in the difficult position of claiming Truth in a world that does not believe in Truth. We call for sacrifice and continence in an environment that glorifies personal freedom and gratification.

Christianity, in our day, is suffering from new and more subtle persecutions than in the past. We are not being burned at the stake or thrown to the lions, as were our forebears. Rather, Christians today are under *ideological persecution*, which is just as strong and potentially even more dangerous to the future of the faith. The world is not interested in the message of Jesus. It does not even want it spoken, lest its demands and its message of sacrifice infringe upon someone's freedom.

THE PARADOX OF RELATIVISTIC TOLERANCE

If the present Christian position sounds grim, should we be surprised? Jesus painted a grim picture for his followers. What hope could they take from his words: "The Son of Man is going to be betrayed into human hands, and they will kill him." (Matt. 17: 22-23) All is not roses in following Christ. The time may soon come when the Church as a whole, as in the early centuries of its existence, must take up its cross and follow him.

Perhaps it is in persecution that the Church will rediscover the unity it has lost. The wide gulfs between different sects that follow Christ are glaringly apparent. If we are persecuted for our morals, it will no longer be Catholic vs. Protestant or one evangelical denomination vs. another. The world will view us as one. Our persecution will, by necessity, unite us.

This challenge of modern culture against the very foundation of the Church may indeed work toward God's purpose in bringing the varying schisms within his flock back into the same fold. *"Blessed are those who are persecuted for righteousness' sake, for theirs is the kingdom of heaven… Rejoice and be glad, for your reward is great in heaven."* (Matt. 5:10-11)

The confidence of the Holy Spirit allows us to take pride in our faith even through the worst persecution the world can muster. When the Spirit of Truth came upon the disciples at Pentecost, they poured into the streets, proclaiming their joy. Only death could stop them. If the hope of Christianity is worth proclaiming, even in the face of death, why fear proclaiming it now when faced merely with the scorn of our peers?

Now, more than ever, is the time to take pride in our faith.

Persecution, ideological now instead of physical, was promised to us just as surely as joy. The world's concept of freedom offers no hope of *ultimate* freedom, for it is founded on no *ultimate* truth. Thus we continue to confidently proclaim our hope. We know where ultimate Freedom and Truth are to be found. *"If you suffer as a Christian, do not consider it a disgrace, but glorify God because you bear this name."* (I Peter 4:16).

Lord God, make me proud to be a Christian. Make me proud to proclaim my hope, even if they call me a fool; proud to follow the way of Christ, the way of the cross. Through charity, compassion and love make me the vessel by which you show what it means to be a Christian.

MAKE IT MINE!

APPLYING THE LESSONS FROM THIS CHAPTER IN MY LIFE:

➤ Have I allowed myself to be seduced by the world's definition of freedom? What seems more attractive: lonely, individualistic freedom or freedom that is united to Christian truth?

➤ Think about what it really means to be free. What thoughts and feelings do you have when you hear that word? Is there fear in the idea of relinquishing control of your life?

➤ Pray honestly for the humility to surrender your individual freedom to God's plan for you. Watch how this new attitude begins to manifest in your life.

PART II:
AN ACCOUNTABLE COMMUNITY

Five: Morality—A Joyful Playground

"The aim of this instruction is love that comes from a pure heart, a good conscience, and sincere faith." - I Timothy 1:5

Many Christians of a philosophical bent find it difficult to submit to the doctrines of Catholicism (or any denomination for that matter), fearing that it will limit the adventures of their minds. For me, however, Catholic doctrine gives me the freedom and safety to explore my thoughts within the confines of a wisdom that has been passed down through the generations, directly from Christ and his apostles.

The last chapter examined the concept of false freedom. This applies also to exercises of the mind.

Secular philosophy would rather start from a point of breaking down past ideas in the quest to find new ones. But I find the construct of the "old" Christian ideas to be highly freeing. Within the comforting principles of Christianity, my mind is truly and safely free to explore.

G. K. Chesterton offers a wise analogy: "Catholic doctrine and discipline may be walls; but they are walls of a playground." Imagine some children playing on the flat grassy top of an island in the sea. So long as there is a wall around the cliff's edge, they can fling themselves into every frantic game with abandon and joy. If the walls were knocked down, however, leaving the naked peril of the precipice, they would then huddle in terror in the center of the island. Their song, and their joy, will have ceased.[10]

What constitutes the walls to this joyful playground? Quite simply, they are made from the morality of Christian teaching. Once again, it is the so called "law"—that which the world sees as a restriction to freedom—which gives us the freedom to live and think to the best of our human abilities. Morality is the societal context for law. It also forms the foundation of the community we call *Religion*.

Here in Part Two, we will first examine morality— its purpose, nature and history. Next, we will look at the need all of us have to be part of a community. These two concepts, morality and community, lead us to the necessity of *Church*. This leads to the question of the relationship between churches. Finally, I will take a more personal turn and relate my reasons for choosing to be part of the Catholic Church.

CHRISTIAN VALUES ARE INGRAINED IN OUR CULTURE

Morality is often viewed as being promulgated by religion; thus, its concept, in word at least, is written off in favor of what is perceived as freedom.

Our society considers *truth,* and therefore also *law,* to be up to the individual to craft for oneself. It shrinks from any creed that names truth and outlines morality. Thus, the concept of "right and wrong" loses meaning. Yet only the utterly lawless and perverse actually dispense with morality. Even devoid of religion, morality's value to a social structure and good personal health is valued. Society continues to function *as if*

---

[10] G. K. Chesterton: *Orthodoxy,* chap 9

there is an absolute to right and wrong, yet *Absolute Truth* is not acknowledged. The morality which society follows is without roots.

The question begs asking: Where did this moral compass come from?

It came directly from the Christian moral teaching which has so influenced, yet also come to be taken for granted in western society.

Earlier, we noted the difficulty of today's Christian, struggling to share the gospel in a world which is already familiar with the message. Few people stop to consider how much Christian teaching is accepted by society at large without a second thought.

Consider the moral concept of *Love your neighbor.* And further, *Love your enemies.* These are totally revolutionary and non-intuitive moral commandments. They go against the human instinct that ruled the primitive world. In such words, there is not a cost/benefit consideration. There is certainly not justice. Yet this has now come to define how we are expected to act, whether or not we accept the religion from which this idea came. This is just one of countless ways Christian morality has influenced the world.

Modern society attempts to disassociate itself from Christian morals while operating within a society based on Judeo-Christian values. Søren Kierkegaard compares the situation to a child who rebels against its parents while unhesitatingly continuing to accept the daily food and shelter its parents provide.[11] The child never grasps the fallacy. Modern society is just like the child when it accepts a value system while rebelling against the source of those values.

---

[11] S. Kierkegaard: *Works of Love,* I, II C

As humanism spread through the western world, some secular philosophers faced this truth. They had to confront the question of what a society without religion would look like. Voltaire, after himself rejecting religion, encouraged Christianity among his servants, fearing the loss of Christian morals would diminish their respect for his authority. Clearly, even Voltaire understood that humanism is intrinsically selfish, while Christianity, and, by extension, religious morals, are intrinsically *un*selfish. It was well enough for Voltaire to believe in a selfish creed, but he recognized that social structure could not allow everyone to live selfishly.

Some scientists fear what will happen if society accepts the non-existence of God, and all its implications, and rejects religion. In a conversation recorded between two of the pioneers of modern physics, Werner Heisenberg and Wolfgang Pauli, they discuss what they see as an eventual and unavoidable rejection of "the parables and images of the old religion." If scientific knowledge leads even the average, unlearned person to reject religious ethics, they fear a complete breakdown in society, even "unimaginable horrors," in Pauli's words.[12]

The fallacy shared by Voltaire and Pauli is that they advocate a different truth for the learned than for the masses. By such an admission, something is necessarily lacking in their professed truth. The Christian view of the world, by contrast, presents a truth valid for all walks of life, all social stations, and all levels of intellect.

---

[12] Werner Heisenberg: *Physics & Beyond: Encounters & Conversations*, chap 7

WHAT CAME FIRST: RELIGION OR MORALITY?

An alternate view of morality places it antecedent to religion. Religion, according to this viewpoint, developed in history as a method of containing humanity's innate sense of right and wrong. By this perspective, even if all religion were abandoned, an ingrained moral compass would persist in each of our hearts, preventing society from spiraling into chaos.

Interestingly, this is similar to what Christianity professes, as does its historic predecessor, Judaism. *Religion,* as we know the concept, did not come into the world until the time of Abraham, yet God implanted right and wrong within the first man and woman. Long before Abraham's time, there were understood consequences upon those who strayed from that code. We can, then, agree that religion came into the world as a tool for refining morality. The atheist believes it was done to regulate social behavior, while the religious believes it came from an innate sense of God's goodness and justice.

Some Christians (notably, C. S. Lewis in *Mere Christianity*) have pointed to an ingrained moral sense as evidence of God's hand in the makeup of every human being. The law of human nature, it is argued, appeals to an understood sense that it is *right* to do good to others and *wrong* to do them harm; to put it even more simply, unselfishness is better than selfishness.

Though this argument is intriguing, on its own, it comes up short, for the unselfishness of doing what is right rather than wrong is vital for any functioning society. Anyone in a position of authority, whether a political ruler or even Voltaire with his servants, has the motivation to promote this "law of human nature" as the just social order. When this order breaks down, so does society. In primitive social structures, morality could even have existed as a tool of survival. Humans knew their success depended on cultivating the companionship and respect of others. It would be beneficial to do good to others to gain the protection of the tribe. As such, morality can just as easily be argued to be a learned law as an ingrained natural sense.

If the sense of right and wrong were a true law of nature, we would see its evidence in the smallest of children, but this is not the case. Indeed, a baby, though we do not blame it, is the most selfish of creatures. It cries and scolds for what it wants and becomes indignant when it does not get its way. As it begins to grow, the child learns its first morality by desiring to avoid punishment or pain. Only over the years does it learn to live by a principal of unselfishness for its own sake. If the child grew to adulthood completely uninfluenced by society and religion, would an unselfish morality ever be learned? By God's mercy, we may hope it would, but the evidence of observation gives no assurance that an unselfish nature would prevail. It is difficult to gain convincing evidence that a sense of right and wrong, free from social influences, is written into our very makeup.

THE POISON OF SELFISHNESS

In the last chapter, we looked at modern society's mistaken concept of freedom. The idolatry of supposed freedom has produced a positively lethal result: selfishness being perceived as a *right*.

The extreme value modern culture has placed on what it defines as "freedom" has led us to a point where selfishness is no longer considered reprehensible. After all, if I have the freedom to do whatever I wish, the current culture would have me believe it is my "right" to pursue every one of my desires. What could be a more apt definition of self-centeredness than this?

Modernism has become so blinded by its pursuit of freedom that it cannot see the blatant absurdity of this claim. What society has come to consider a "right" is in fact nothing less than pure selfishness.

Humanity is one community. Every individual is dependent to some extent on every other. The moment selfishness begins to dominate motive and behavior, we take away both the freedom and life's blessings from others. In seeking to possess good things—to hoard them at the expense of others—goodness itself becomes perverted.

The world excuses selfishness by calling it freedom. I would rather know it by its true name, and recognize it for what it really is. How truly did St. Augustine write, "All the good that you love is from the creator, but unjustly is it loved if God be forsaken for it."[13]

We are meant to enjoy the things that give pleasure to our hearts and bodies. The joy that is brought from well-earned pleasure is a wonderful blessing, but we only feel the reward if we also seek to share that joy with others. By seeking the good of others along with ours own, pleasure will be fulfilled.

This is pleasure encased in moral law. What is good for the whole will also prove good for each individual. Personal gratification need not be forsaken, but rather subordinated to the gratification of others.

Exaltation of selfish aims over the good of others is the cause of most of the evil in the world.

---

[13] St. Augustine: *Confessions*, IV, 18

PLATO AND MORALITY AS JUSTICE

Even in society at large, where morality benefits the group as a whole, the cause and effect brought on by selfishness is not necessarily intuitive. Human will is more disposed toward selfishness, seeking comfort and pleasure at the expense of others.

Scripture give several examples of early humanity's failure to incorporate morality into its societal norms. Before the flood, *"The Lord saw that the wickedness of humankind was great in the earth, and that every inclination of the thoughts of their hearts was evil."* (Gen. 5:5) Looking upon the wicked cities of Sodom and Gomorrah, The Lord said *"How very grave is their sin!"* (Gen. 18:20). These stories show that morality was expected of humanity long before religion was established. God gave religion to Abraham, and from him it spread through the world. Although we can see how morality benefits society, history's example shows that we are still more inclined toward selfishness unless moral law is given.

This law can come in two forms—as religion or as socially instituted justice.

On the subject of justice within the state, the defining work of literature is Plato's *Republic*. In this monumental work, he paints a picture of a functioning society maintained by a balanced understanding of justice. Plato understood both that human nature is disposed toward selfishness and that a perfectly moral individual will ultimately be ridiculed and outcast. Thus he advocates justice within a state as the means for promoting morality. For Plato, *The State* was analogous to *Religion*. The state was so important to Plato's philosophy that Socrates willingly became a martyr to the state when he chose death over banishment from

Athens, the reasoning for which is described in the dialogue *Crito*. Socrates drank the poisonous hemlock because, more than the cause he had championed, he valued the structure of justice by which he was sentenced.

Yet this very act of Socrates shows how the philosophy was lacking. Socrates was condemned because he revolted against what he perceived as *injustice* in the state. Ultimately justice within the state must be finely balanced. Any disruption (or *cor*ruption) can quickly unravel the moral foundation. We see this clearly in the early human societies described in Genesis.

Justice as constructed by a state cannot, by definition, be absolute. For within justice, there always remains the possibility of a power vacuum. This is graphically apparent in the modern world. Francis Schaeffer identifies this power vacuum as "the loss of the Christian consensus which originally gave us form and freedom in [western society.]"[14] Justice becomes either rudderless or like the hypocritical child described by Kierkegaard. Morality, therefore, cannot find its ideal model within Platonic philosophy. True morality demands a higher calling.

THE COMMUNAL GOOD

Whether morality is an ingrained sense, a learned law, or a tool of justice, its value would be foolish to argue. However, we believe it came to the human community, and, whatever it might tell us about God, the simple reality is that over time, doing good will have a better result for the individual and the society

---

[14] Francis Schaeffer: *How Should We Then Live?*, chap 11

than doing ill. Even the most selfish individual, if wise with foresight, can see that if he is to achieve his selfish goals, *un*selfishness must be incorporated into his actions. If an individual never exercises goodness toward his fellows, his subsequent isolation will frustrate his selfish intent.

Morality is a code of action designed to put the good of others in line with our individual good. Thus, morality is not a concept that can be discussed in isolation. It requires others to complete it. Morality deals with a community. Our experience confirms that the good of the community leads to the good of the individual. To steal may be good for me, but it is bad for the community. I avoid the immoral act of theft because I know that a breakdown in social order and trust will impact negatively on me as well. Such action is detrimental to the community of which I am a part.

This is not to be confused with Plato's concept of justice within the state. Justice and morality are often equated, but their meanings are different. Justice is legislated downward from authority. Morality is motivated from the individual, upward to the full community. Justice contains no love. Morality reaches its highest state through love.

As we have seen, modern society values freedom to an irrational degree. Morality is often seen as an obstruction to freedom. Religion is viewed as an enemy of pleasure. What religion attempts to convey, however, is that morality, while restricting some freedoms in the short term, prevents one from becoming a slave to selfishness. Furthermore, the individual freedoms and quests for pleasure we have come to value cause much of the pain and chaos in the world.

In primitive and oppressive societies, the strong have freedom and the weak have none. Modern culture, through its glorification of freedom, has created the same dichotomy. Unless freedom is enjoined with other principles, it becomes meaningless. What the strong call freedom, the weak call oppression. Morality is the law which, to modern culture, may appear as a limitation to freedom, but whose goal is a shared freedom for all—strong and weak, rich and poor—for the betterment of the human race as a whole.

A Pathway to Love

Looking upon morality as a restriction is to miss its essence. Truly, morality is a guide to greater freedom, greater enjoyment of life, and greater love. It builds the walls around the playground of life.

Immoral deeds, which go against our understood natural moral law, may bring immediate pleasure but leave us sadly unfulfilled afterward. The consequences often lead to despair.

God did not give us moral law to test us, but rather because he loves us. He knows with perfect foresight how much happier we will be if we follow his design. Morality is a law of love. Following a moral law for any other reason than love is not true morality. It is only justice—a lower virtue. St. Augustine said, "All of God's commandments are embraced in love… Every commandment has love for its aim. But whatever is done either through fear of punishment, or from some other motive, is not done as it ought to be done, however it may appear to men."[15]

---

[15] St. Augustine: *Enchiridion*. 121

Moral law is a gift from God, guiding us toward a life of happiness, health, and peace. In considering the good of our neighbors along with our own, morality also becomes our gift to our community.

Religion gives a framework for morality, but it gives something else as well. It answers the question of "why." Why is it good to be unselfish? Why is it good to be loving? Why is virtue admirable?

Religious morality is the roadmap to the achievement of our desires.

The greatest desire of our hearts is love. Love is more important to us than life itself. In Christianity, we are told that our God not only loves us, but in fact *is* love! By practicing unselfish morality, we are acting with love toward others. Knowing that moral law was given to us by God, we should trust that God knows what is best for us, and that our greatest joy comes from following the very law under which we often chafe.

Even in a purely atheistic society, it is easy to see how giving love is the only way to receive love. Christianity exemplifies this truth on a far grander scale. Believing in a God who is love, we are assured that our love and compassion are rewarded by a greater reciprocating love than we can possibly imagine.

This promise is at the heart of the message Jesus came to earth to share. He instituted a moral code but constantly affirmed that his creed was not based on justice, but rather on love.

Once again, we Christians have missed the point in our relationship with the world. By couching morality in a set of rules, we have pushed the world toward rejection. Rather, we should proclaim with delight the truly liberating nature of morality. It is only by giving up certain freedoms that we can truly become free. Morality contains a salvific quality—not in that by following a set of rules we will attain salvation eventually, but that we will achieve the salvation of happiness and peace *right now*.

Lord God, bind me to your timeless truths. Let me accept limited freedom with joy, in the trust that you know and want only the best for my life.

MAKE IT MINE!

APPLYING THE LESSONS FROM THIS CHAPTER IN MY LIFE:

➤ Do I act morally only because it is the law (either of society or Christianity) or do I do it out of love? Why or why not?

➤ Think about all the ways an action you take may influence others—either positively or negatively. Think about it on both a local and global scale. How does this awareness change your desire for things?

➤ Consider the free actions you want to take throughout the day and week. Would such actions take freedom away from someone else, even in a small way? Can you remember a time when someone else took an action which took away your freedom?

Six: Our Deep Need For One Another

"Truly I tell you, if two of you agree on earth about anything you ask, it will be done for you by my Father in heaven. For where two or three are gathered in my name, I am there among them." - Matthew 18:19-20

Jesus prescribed a moral program that marks a path to lasting joy. This joy is found through the good we do toward one another. Thus, morality only makes sense within a community. It is clear that by doing good for others within my community, I am doing good for myself. Yet we do not always take seriously just how important the good of our community is to each one of us.

The community of the human race is the primary thing that validates each of our own realities. Without the interaction of others, we lose a grasp on ourselves. We need one another on a very basic level. Companionship is one of our greatest comforts, and the loss of it is a dreadful fear. We highly value our families and friends, even mere acquaintances, and greatly bemoan their loss. Humanity has a great fear of being alone. Other than death, this may be our greatest fear. Indeed, much of our fear of death stems from our fear of aloneness.

Since the beginning of our history, we have sought one another in community. Companionship has been vital to the survival of our race. From the intimate (marriage, family) to the local (clan, tribe, or, in modern times, co-workers and groups of friends) to the national and finally global levels, we rely on one another for success, and we expect others to behave in predictable ways.

This network comes alive through the practice of morality.

AN INTERTWINED WORLD

Our lives are intertwined in a fantastic and beautiful framework. Daily, we count on the work performed by others, just as they count on ours. The community of our groups and cities and globe work so smoothly that we take it for granted. But if one chain is broken, chaos ensues, leading to strikes, riots, famine, and war.

From this perspective, our work—our participation in the community of our world—is perhaps our most basic act of love. By providing our talents to the community, we give a gift and accept the gifts of others. It is a simple exchange of love. If other people are this important to me, then we must recognize that the good of the community equates directly to our own wellbeing. This is where morality comes into play.

Love is the greatest of all human desires, yet it is one desire that I cannot possibly fulfill on my own. Love necessitates another. Only by giving love can I receive love. The ability to give—the inclination toward unselfishness—is therefore the only way to come into possession of my greatest desire.

Because of our dependence on love, we are necessarily a *community people*. Community provides both moral accountability and the opportunity to love. My acts of love benefit the community. Reciprocally, the community has tremendous power to refresh and renew me. This is true at every level of relationship, from the intimate to the global.

COMMUNITY'S GIVE AND TAKE

Love is communion—it cannot be experienced alone. It exists between friends, lovers or even strangers who treat each other with goodness. Love is void without another to share it.

Love must be given if it is to be received. Love between two people is never complete until both parties give of themselves. Yet love does not ask for reciprocation; it is in the offering of itself that love is fulfilled.

This free and total gift of love is also called compassion. We exist in the community of humanity together. If one person suffers, the rest should respond with compassion.

In our compassion and in our charity, it is imperative to recognize that we could just as easily find ourselves on the other side. There is a thin line between those who need charity and those who give it. The forces that hold one in the more prosperous plane are extremely fickle. If I resent giving charity now, when I am able, who will be there to help me when I am thrown into poverty or despair? Compassion and charity are two-way streets. My whole life may be spent on only one side of the street, but that can change with alarming speed. If I have lived selfishly, who will have sympathy for me in my need?

If my longing is fulfilled by *giving* love, then equally important is being able to open myself to *receive* the love of others. This is harder than it would seem. Our pride often makes us reluctant to accept the very love we know will satisfy our longing.

An example of the necessary give and take of charity was when Jesus washed the feet of his friends. In the culture of that time, a teacher would *never* have done this for his disciples. Peter's response of "Lord, you will never wash my feet!" is what we would expect them all to say. This was quite a scandal. But Jesus did this for two specific reasons: First, to show them that to be great in love, one must offer loving service to others. Secondly, as he told Peter, you must be able to accept the love which is offered to you.

"You call me teacher and Lord," he told them, *"and you are right, for that is what I am. So if I, your Lord and teacher, have washed your feet, you also ought to wash one another's feet. For I have set you an example, that you also should do as I have done to you."* (John 13: 13-15) Not even Judas, his betrayer, was excluded from the love of foot-washing. If Jesus could do such a service for the one whom he knew would betray him to his death, we should be able to do such service for one another.

I often find myself with Peter, more comfortable as the giver than the receiver. I experience this with my peers. I cannot imagine the strength of my protest if Jesus Christ stooped to wash my feet!

It can feel uncomfortable to accept the charity, gifts, or services I feel I did not earn. If I will not accept them, however, then I am doing a disservice not only to myself, but to the giver. Furthermore, what right have I to refuse a simple service from a friend, loved one, or stranger, when I accept my very life, undeserved and freely given by God? God, as the first giver, desires that we continue to give… and receive…

via generosity and charity. This process, in its many forms, is community.

Community reveals the living, breathing give-and-take of charitable love.

HUMANITY'S GREATEST DESIRE

Every person with whom we share the human condition is a potential vessel of love. We can unlock this love through a vigilance of compassion, readying ourselves for charity whenever and wherever the need arises.

We value love even more than life itself. Yet our search for it often leaves us empty. Even if we are diligent in our offerings of love and compassion, and free with charity for those in need, our love may not be reciprocated. Thus, even these virtues can lead to disappointment.

Rather than losing heart, the Christian believes in a God who created us out of love and can bring us into a perfect experience of love—a perfect community to be shared with all the saints.

Am I speaking of a heaven that can only be unlocked with death? Quite the contrary! I am speaking of a blessing which is here right now. The only key to unlocking this blessing is love. If we can truly live with love, sharing our blessings and accepting the blessings of the community, we do not have to wait for an afterlife. Heaven begins now. Love is our greatest desire, and love is available to all, if only we break the lock of selfishness.

RELIGION IS COMMUNITY

Of all the characteristics of organized religion, I believe that the most important are community and accountability. Ultimately, it is the community which provides and maintains accountability.

The communion of humanity validates each one of us individually. From the earliest history, peoples identified themselves in the context of their community. Humanity can hardly even be defined without the interaction of others in a community. Morality and justice relate to the good of this community. It is community which provides the opportunity to love.

Religion, at its fundamental level, is a community. We need others to provide accountability. A religious community holds a collection of individuals together, through accountability and supported by doctrine. Religion, as such, should not be confused with virtue, which is the practice of following morality, with or without religious practice.

It is not only the present community which makes up a religious body. We can draw on the community that has upheld the religion since the beginning.

The Catholic Church speaks of a *deposit of faith*, by which Christians of today are supported by the faith that has blossomed throughout Christian history. Indeed, we are supported by the faith of God's people since the beginning of time. The writer of Hebrews says that we are surrounded by a great cloud of witnesses to the truth. (Heb. 12:1) Some of the early faithful—the Apostles, Saints and Doctors—are remembered for passing on their faith experiences to us. But it is the entire history of Christianity that generates this *deposit of faith*, strengthening each generation anew.

The vital importance of religion thus is made clear. Without its structure and the support of those who came before, we risk growing lax in the practice of our beliefs. We need the accountability of our religious community.

No religion is without flaw, for every religion relies on an infrastructure established and developed by humans. But though flawed, each religion attempts to establish a method for moral existence. Certainly, many men and women have lived virtuous lives without the constraints and dogmas of organized churches. I admire such pilgrims, but few possess the strength to embark on that path without being tempted away. For the majority of believers, it is the support of a religious community that gives the strength and fortitude to follow their beliefs.

Accountability and community are the fundamental reasons for organized religion. Yes, God and righteousness can be reached in solitude, but it is a difficult, dangerous road.

One of my favorite gospel stories is from the second chapter of Mark, when Jesus was preaching in a crowded room. A paralytic was brought on a mat but could not get close to Jesus because of the crowds. The paralyzed man had no hope on his own to get through to the healer, so his friends took him to the roof, cut a hole in it and lowered him down on his mat, right in front of Jesus. Jesus, not minding the interruption, happily healed the man. This is a great example of religious community in action. The man did not have the strength to come to Jesus himself, but a community of believers defied the odds to bring him there.

Similarly, when we go through times of emotional and spiritual paralysis, it may take a community to lower us down on our mat to the feet of God. Without community, we would struggle to crawl there ourselves, and we might lack the strength to get through.

AN ACCOUNTABLE COMMUNITY

Religion offers us a community of people, sharing love and holding one another accountable as they strive to follow a shared morality. Religion recognizes how the morality discussed in the previous chapter benefits both the individual and the whole. Without the structure of religion and the support of the community, it is easy for one to lose track of the moral code. Accountability and community are the fundamental reasons for the importance of religion. It may be possible to follow the path of love and charity and to point ourselves toward our divine aspirations without religion, but it is far more difficult.

Through the shared principles of morality, religion has become a vessel of charity in the world. The very first Christian writer, St. Paul, identified charity as one of the pre-eminent tasks of the Church. *"As you excel in everything,"* he told the Corinthians, *"so we want you to excel also in this generous undertaking."* (II Corin. 8:7) The Church of the immediately succeeding centuries well understood the place of charitable works in the very validity of the church. During the Third Century persecution of Christians in Rome, Deacon Lawrence was ordered to hand over all the treasure of the Church to the authorities. Lawrence distributed all the Church's funds to the poor and then presented the poor themselves as the real treasure of the church.[16]

In the early days of Christendom, charity was fundamental to life as a follower of Jesus. We are told that they lived for a while in an ideal community, for *"there was not a needy person among them, for as many as owned lands or houses sold them and brought the proceeds of what was sold. They laid it at the apostles' feet, and it was distributed to each as any had need."* (Acts 4:34-35) The Christian community is now larger, but we are still compelled to live with love and charity toward those who share this name. As the centuries have unfolded, organized charity has become one of the fundamental works of a church body. The Catholic Church established the first hospitals and the first orphanages in the world. Today it takes a leading role in disaster relief and the effort to ease hunger in the world.

Pope Benedict XVI, in Part II of his encyclical, *Deus Caritas Est,* gave strong and challenging support to those working in charitable organizations under the name of the Church, following the first example of the apostles, that *"all who believed were together and had all things in common."* (Acts 2:44) By these words, it is inconceivable to withhold charity.

His predecessor, Pope John Paul II, makes a clear distinction between the work carried out by the community as a whole (charitable organizations), which involves "larger tasks, requiring cooperation and the use of technical means," and "individual activity, especially by people who are better prepared for it in regard to the various kinds of human suffering which can only be alleviated in an individual or personal

---

[16] St. Ambrose: *De officiis ministrorum*, II, 28, 140

way." [17] While a community (the Church) has an intrinsic role in, to use John Paul's definition, "the work of human solidarity," each of us must be equally prepared to give our love at a moment's notice, in the same way that we would hope for others to give theirs in our own time of need.

Religion is merely the form given to a community of love. Morality is the roadmap for a community to function in love.

THE REVOLUTIONARY MORALITY OF JESUS

I am a Christian because of Jesus—because of the promise of love he gave to the world.

This motivates me to follow the specific morality he taught. My calling and obligation is to live with virtue, to love others through charity and compassion, and to show respect for our creator. This is what Jesus commanded us to do.

Within this context, what is the place for religious practice? Jesus never commanded his followers to "go to church," but rather to "love your neighbor." John the Presbyter put our task simply in saying: "Whoever does good is from God; whoever does evil has not seen God. Do not imitate what is evil, but imitate what is good." (III John, 11) This commandment speaks not of an organized church; neither does it leave room to claim that one church is greater than another. John says that we may recognize the good person by the good works he or she does. Any other claim is hollow.

So where is the place of church? Can my good works—my "imitation of good"—be just as well achieved without such structure?

---

[17] Pope John Paul II: *Salvifici Doloris*, VII, 29

JESUS' TWOFOLD MESSAGE

An honest spiritual journey takes us into our own consciences with a true evaluation of what we believe to be right and wrong. For me, these questions are authoritatively answered in the person of Jesus.

The moral program he established in the world was completely revolutionary. It gave people an entirely new way to interact with one another and with God. Jesus painted a sublime portrait of love and compassion for all humanity. Love is the glue that holds the entirety of Christian morality together.

The teachings of Jesus can be summed up in two main points, both derived from the Hebrew Scriptures, but expanded upon in his ministry. One is the instruction to "love your neighbor as you love yourself." (Lev. 19:18) The other was to show people that God is love (Psalm 36). These two principles must be paramount in our attitude toward the world, affecting everything we do in life as Christians.

People tend to get caught up in the rules and regulations of Christianity. Jesus' two principles are often pushed aside by minor details and dogma. I am reminded of when Father Michael Ryan of Seattle encountered a college student who asked him how many laws the Catholic Church had. He jovially responded that the Church had recently paired down to around eighteen hundred laws. The young student asked him: "Why does the Catholic Church have so many laws when Jesus only had two?" Father Ryan could only respond, "Touché!" [18] This is a good reminder for all doctrinized Catholics as well as Protestants. If any would endeavor to be a good

---

[18] Fr. Michael Ryan: Sermon at St. James Cathedral, Seattle, 2005

Christian, their task is to follow the two rules of Jesus—love God and love one another. Everything else will fall into place.

DOES CHRISTIANITY STILL FOLLOW CHRIST?

But wait! If my goal is to follow Jesus Christ, not Christianity, *per se*, then where is the place for *religion*? It seems to be extraneous. Might there be another way to achieve the moral accountability we seek in Catholicism? Jesus had a community yet seemed to condemn organized religion at every turn.

The pomp of priestly orders, the lavish costumes, wealth and excess of the Vatican, has nothing to do with Jesus. It eerily resembles the Jewish hierarchy of his day, whom he called "a brood of vipers!" There are many in the Church today who would do well to heed Jesus' warnings. The truest followers of Jesus are doing the work of compassion and love in the world.

Pope Francis, since his election, has given signs of hope that the leadership of the Church is finally beginning to embrace its true purpose of servitude to the body of Christ. He understands and embraces Pope Gregory I's description of the papal role: *Servus servorum Dei*, "The servant of the servants of God."

It will take a great deal of strength for Pope Francis to make the reforms to the inner workings of the Vatican where Benedict failed. But Francis has approached his papacy with an attitude of humility. As the image of the Church to the world, this attitude has the potential to do more good than any tangible reforms.

Despite its flaws, the Catholic Church gives structure to the teachings of Jesus. It continues to offer accountability and community, creating a framework through which the faithful can live the morality taught by Jesus.

The argument is often made that Jesus himself did not belong to a church; he spent most of his public ministry bucking religious authority. The gospels portray his life quite differently. Early in his ministry, he submitted faithfully to the religious practice in which he was raised. He even had the authority to teach as a Rabbi in the Synagogues. He never stopped following the customs of Judaism—his religion. Jesus did not rebuke the religious structure until he had earned the right through years of studying its ways and learning its teachings at the feet of those same scribes and Pharisees. Toward the end of his life, the religious leaders abandoned him. Even then, once he embarked on a ministry that no longer fit under Jewish religious authority, his first act was to gather a community around himself. This became his church. He needed people just like we do. There was nothing solitary about Jesus' spiritual journey, and he exhorted his followers to remain united after he was gone.

Dreaming that the Christian message can thrive without structure is just that—a dream. Jesus may have criticized religious structure, but he still laid the groundwork for the Church which would follow him, complete with leadership (Matt. 16:18, John 21: 15-17) and what developed into apostolic succession (John 17:16-19, Acts 1:21-26). If Jesus appeared today, he would have strong words for the corruptions of current Christianity, both Catholic and Protestant. But the structure itself is valuable. It holds the faithful together.

Religion is community, and community is an environment for love.

Without love, religion is in vain. Without love, *life* is in vain.

I come to you, Lord, strengthened by the community of believers and saints from every age. Let me be generous and compassionate in sharing the light of Christ with those I meet.

MAKE IT MINE!

APPLYING THE LESSONS FROM THIS CHAPTER IN MY LIFE:

➤ What does the concept of Church mean to me? Is it merely a building or is it a true community of moral support?

➤ Think about the ways your community supports you. You are likely a member of many communities: family, work, church, team, etc. What would your life be like without these communities?

➤ Pope John Paul II called each Christian individual to participate in the "work of human solidarity." Look for a tangible opportunity in the coming days to bring Christian love into another person's life.

Seven: In Search Of Lost Unity

"I am the good shepherd. The good shepherd lays down
his life for the sheep. I have other sheep that do not belong
to this fold. I must bring them also, and they will listen to
my voice." - John 10:11, 16

The importance of organized religion is clear, but is one necessarily better than another? Surely community and accountability can be found in all religions.

The primary factor that steers most individuals into one religion rather than another, or one denomination of Christianity over the other, is family and culture. The vast majority of people who seek God will do it within the context of their formative education. God surely wants to reach people within this context. It seems unthinkable that he would condemn anyone for failing to break free from these first influences. Yet this is the stance taken by many people.

While I believe strongly in the tenets of Catholicism, I believe in a God eager to reach humanity in any way he can.

When Gandhi was asked why, when he admired Christianity, he did not convert to it, he is said to have replied, "Hinduism is my path. If we are all climbing to the same mountaintop, does it matter by which path we climb?" Perhaps it does not matter as much as we have been conditioned to think. This metaphor still leaves the question of whether some paths might be easier than others. But even if one path is easier, the easiest is not necessarily the most direct. When climbing a mountain, the most direct route is actually the steepest.

I believe that a relationship with God can be carved from any religious structure. At the Second Vatican Council, the Catholic Church finally agreed, indicating that Christianity was the best, most direct path, but that other paths could also lead to God.[19]

This acknowledgement of the intrinsic good found in many religions does not lessen our responsibility to seek truth and follow it. Religious choice is no longer strictly bound in culture. We have more opportunity to explore various religions than at any other time in history. Our present age glorifies religious choice as it seeks to relativize the truth. Within this context, religious choice seems a less serious decision. In reality it is greater. It is a solemn decision that must be taken very seriously.

TRAGIC DISCORD

Religion, at its most basic level, is community, and community—literally *cum unity*—is an act of living with love. Every truth in religion can always be brought back to love.

How then, did religion come to represent so much discord in the world?

Surely little grieves God so much as the discord among those who follow him. Discord has no place in true religion.

The rifts between religions are often tragically minute. The original break between Orthodoxy and

---

[19] Vatican II: *Lumen Gentium*, 16

Catholicism was for geographical reasons. Emperor Constantine established a second capital city. When Constantinople grew in strength, Rome sought a political alliance with Charlemagne's central European kingdom, thus completing the break. The rift between Catholics and Protestants during the Reformation was wider, but time has rendered many of the differences obsolete. In Europe, the pain of murder, wars and persecution makes peace difficult, but where the history does not exist, there is little reason for discord. As a Protestant leader in Cameroon told Pope John Paul II, "We know we are divided, but we do not know why."[20] If history and superficiality could be scraped away, Christians of all walks might wonder the same thing: "Why are we divided?"

Protestant reformers broke away from Catholicism over disputes they were willing to die for. After a few decades of power, however, Protestant leaders were committing many of the same atrocities the Catholics had done to their predecessors. The Protestants eagerly killed heretics after their founders were killed as heretics by the Catholics, who in turn had built their faith on the apostles who were killed as heretics, who followed Jesus who was… killed as a heretic.

Naturally, the Christian unity of the first years after Jesus' life could not last. Much as we now glorify the early days of Christendom, discord crept in quickly. Paul opened his first letter to the Corinthians saying *"It has been reported to me that there are quarrels among you… Each of you says 'I belong to Paul,' or 'I belong to Apollos' or 'I belong to Cephas… Has Christ been divided? Was Paul crucified for you? Were you baptized in the name of Paul?"* (I

---

[20] Pope John Paul II: *Crossing the Threshold of Hope*, chap 21

Corin. 1:11-13) There are many names in today's Christendom we could insert instead of Paul and make the same appeal! Much as we respect certain teachers or teachings, they can never replace Christ or Christ's teachings.

The Acts of the Apostles describe many points of disagreement between Peter and Paul, the two primary leaders of the early Church. But their differences paled in comparison to their unity, which brought them both to prison in Rome. Tradition has it that they worked together to strengthen the local Christian community before each being executed.

Persecution created an environment where unity was essential. Thus, the Church's most unified time came in the subsequent centuries under the brutal persecution of Rome. Once Christianity became a political state, discord inevitably followed.

The lust for power always undermines the teachings of Christ.

CHRISTIANITY'S LOST UNITY

Jesus said: *"Where two or three are gathered in my name, I am there among them."* (Matt. 18:20) In these words exists no endorsement of one true church or one true method of worship. The only requirement is that the followers of Jesus gather in his name. He did not say, "Where two or three are gathered under the authority of the Roman Papacy…" He did not say, "Where two or three are gathered and hold no heresy…" He did not say, "Where two or three are gathered and believe this or that, or don't believe this and that about my mother…"

These words of Jesus present the clearest admonishment in the whole Bible against Christian

74

discord, yet the rifts remain. Christians no longer burn other Christians at the stake, but the hatred can be nearly as vicious. I have been told by some Christians that I am not a Christian at all, and am damned to hell because I choose to worship in a different denomination. Those Christians who make such outlandish and self-righteous claims are like the Apostle John who said *"Master, we saw someone casting out demons in your name, and we tried to stop him, because he does not follow with us."* Jesus' words to today's Catholics, Protestants, and Orthodox would be the same as they were then: *"Do not stop him; for whoever is not against you is for you."* (Luke 9:49-50)

Pope John XXIII said that what separates us as believers in Christ is much less than what unites us. On this hope, the Catholic Church has made outreaches like never before to Orthodox and Protestant churches. More work remains, however, as the effort is as political as it is spiritual.

It bears repeating: The differences that have caused these great rifts in Christendom are laughably small. Compassion and love are not at question. Jesus' status as Messiah and Son of God are agreed. At issue are comparatively minor dogmas that have little to no effect on our daily lives. You could lay all the churches of Christianity on the table and, after scraping away the chaff, you would find the same kernel of truth in each of them. Love's work can flourish in all.

INDIVISIBLY CHRISTIAN

Does one sect represent a truer expression of Christianity? I do not know. In fact, the first and only thing I will claim to know in life is that my knowledge is limited. Truth is elusive. Anyone, or any church, that claims absolute theological certainty is on dangerous ground. Thus I do not pose the question: "Does my church represent the truest expression of Christianity?" Rather, I ask: "Does my church provide the best environment for me to continue my journey of discovering Christ's truth?"

I would never presume to claim that my choice is "right" at the expense of another who follows the same Christ. Catholicism has given me a fuller and more personal relationship with God. But I would be a fool to claim a deeper understanding of Christianity than my Protestant parents, two of the wisest Christians I know. Rather, in ecumenism, I draw continually from their wisdom while also drawing from the wisdom of the Catholic Church.

Similarly, I draw from the wisdom of Protestant theologians in almost equal measure to Catholic ones. In the last few chapters I have referenced Søren Kierkegaard, C. S. Lewis and Francis Schaeffer, all Protestants who have had great influence upon my personal belief system. Let me add to them the profound influence of my own father upon my theological formation.

It is important to remember that we are first Christians; only afterwards may we define ourselves as Catholic, Protestant, or Orthodox, if we need to define ourselves at all.

The problem with any dialogue about unity is that all parties seemingly agree, saying: "Yes. Let us be united," but the clause is always "let the others come over to my way of thinking." Obviously this goes nowhere. The starting point must be the kernel of truth affirmed by all branches of Christianity. Where two or three are gathered in the name of God's love, God is there. Where compassion and charity are practiced, truth is there.

The path to our lost unity is in recognition that we are all seeking to do the work of God's love. The Protestant must acknowledge that the Catholic's preferred method of worship is valid, and *vice versa*. The differences are more preference of practice than anything else. The Protestant dislikes the Catholic and Orthodox doctrine of the Communion of Saints, especially the symbols used in this form of prayer. They call it heresy and idolatry, but this is just one of the ways Catholics and Orthodox feel close to God. The goal (closeness to God) is the same in all these sects. If one person is more comfortable reaching that goal in a particular way or in a particular church, unity demands respect for that choice. Radhakrishnan, the great Hindu teacher, has some good advice for Christians when he writes that: "those who love their sects more than truth end by loving themselves more than their sects."[21]

Even theological differences have little bearing on the daily work of Christians in the world.

Let me emphasize again: Truth cannot be treated as relative. That is not the meaning of ecumenism. I strongly believe in the basic tenets of Catholicism. I know wise and righteous men and women of other denominations who feel just as strongly about their own doctrinal beliefs. True ecumenism means respectful dialogue, not full agreement.

For example, I believe some of the doctrines of Mormonism are mistaken and heretical. But as I discovered when I recently sat next to a Mormon on a ten-hour flight from Rome to Cincinnati, our

---

[21] Radhakrishnan: *The Hindu View of Life*, chap 2

similarities, as John XXIII said, were much greater than our differences. Our conversation focused on Jesus' divinity and Christian charity—points on which we wholeheartedly agreed.

In our world, it is impossible to think that our desire for Christian unity will result in one united church structure. We are too different as human beings and far too stubborn. The dialogue I had with the Mormon, just like John Paul II's conversation with the Protestant in Cameroon, should serve as an example of true ecumenism. We are indeed one Church; we all follow Jesus Christ. The point of ecumenical dialogue is not to laboriously discuss our similarities, but to acknowledge and accept our differences. Then perhaps the Catholic and the Protestant can live side by side, worshiping in their own ways, but working together to spread love and compassion in the world. Who knows; we might even learn something from each other!

MY FOOLISH HOPE

Unity does not stop with Christianity. Jews and Muslims, along with Christians, hold the same truth as the fundamental point of their religion—that all were created in the image and with the blessing of God. Disputes should come when the most basic things are disagreed upon, not that which follows. The Buddhist and the Hindu do not believe in a Creating God *per se*, yet value love and compassion just as much as the religions that do. The goal of religion remains the same. Why have the Christian and the Muslim spent a millennium at war when their similarities are much greater than either with an Atheist? The God which made everyone accepts the differences between us. Why can't we?

Strongly as I believe in the Catholic way, I also know that I will be wrong about some things. It would be foolish to pretend I will not. In any matter of knowledge, only a fool trumpets his knowledge in the presence of an expert. In matters of religion, or indeed in all matters of this world, everything we know pales in comparison to the knowledge of he who created everything. Some of the arguments I have spent years formulating and strengthening will break down in the face of God's clear truth. I endeavor to remain humble about my viewpoints, just as I would in the presence of anyone who knows more than I.

I have learned that no matter how well thought out and formed my opinions are, I cannot convince anyone of my position unless they *want* to believe it. Meanwhile, by remaining open minded, my grasp on truth strengthens. An open mind is the only way to learn. The fear of being wrong is the quickest way to close the mind and block knowledge. Even when I firmly believe, I respect those who disagree with me. What unites us is much greater than what separates us.

I have a hope which may be unreasonable optimism. I believe in the potential for ecumenism between all the divergent sects of Christianity, and even all religions, whether or not they believe in Jesus, or God, or even if they only believe in the value of good for its own sake. I think for all of us, our similarities are greater than our differences. As Ghandi said, we are all climbing the same mountain. We would get there faster if we helped each other along rather than fought to get everyone in line with our path.

We are all made in the image of God. We share the same passions and desires and are burdened with the same despairs. These similarities are much stronger than the fact that one of us is a Protestant and one is Catholic, that one is a Buddhist and the other a Muslim. We were all created with the same care, and our longing is for the same love.

Lord God, you love everyone with the same intimate care. Help us to put aside the pride that divides us and humbly unite in your love.

MAKE IT MINE!

APPLYING THE LESSONS FROM THIS CHAPTER IN MY LIFE:

➤ Have I allowed overconfidence in my beliefs and opinions to close my mind?

➤ How do you feel when in the presence of people of different viewpoints or of a different religion? Pray for the wisdom and humility to listen openly to ideas and view of others.

➤ The next time you are conversing with someone of a different religious conviction, make a point of listening more than you speak. Try to learn rather than convince.

Eight: This Is Personal

"Since we are surrounded by so great a cloud of witnesses, let us lay aside every weight and the sin that clings so closely, and let us run with perseverance the race that is set before us, looking to Jesus, the pioneer and perfecter of our faith." - Hebrews 12:1, 2

The words I have just written on religious unity—specifically my desire for understanding and acceptance between various Christian and even non-Christian perspectives—opens a potential "Pandora's box" of tricky questions. I have been adamant not to let truth become relative, yet there are some who see my ecumenical perspective as just that.

It is fair to ask: If all religions have value and if all religious paths have the potential to lead to God, what is the point of following Jesus' teachings at all? Why endure the difficulties of the Christian journey? The eschatological question becomes even more difficult. This perspective, at first, appears to water down the seriousness of heaven and hell. Did all the martyrs die in vain?

In light of these objections, the best I can do is to recount my own spiritual journey, which provides a living example of ecumenism. Paradoxically, my belief in the inherent *good* of all religions and the inherent *truth* of all Christian denominations compelled me to choose a particular one—Catholicism. It is that choice which I will now share.

Catholicism, for me, was definitely a *choice*.

Though I have been a *Christian* my whole life, I have only been *Catholic* since adulthood.

STEEPED IN ECUMENISM

I grew up as a Protestant (though from no specific denomination). My parents were and continue to be among the primary Christian influences in my life. My father (himself a prolific author) taught me to be a thinker and a seeker. I must credit him for training me to be the kind of man who could make the free and informed choice of joining the Catholic Church, even though this choice exposed some theological differences between us. He and I still discuss theology regularly.

My parents taught me and my brothers strict absolutes in the areas of behavior, morality, and ethics. With regard to theology and ideas, they wanted us to think for ourselves and ultimately to *choose* our own lives with Christ. Thus, I never felt that I stepped away from one tradition by embracing a new one. Rather, I still call upon my Protestant knowledge, giving me a broader view of Christianity as a whole.

My parents believed strongly in religious unity. My passion for ecumenism springs directly from their teaching. Our household was always one that encouraged thoughtful inquiry and respect for varying viewpoints, sometimes dramatically so.

I will never forget one incredible night, a few days before my twelfth birthday. A group of twenty-some Chinese college students residing in Canada had been coming to my family home each year as part of their annual trip through the United States. This year, the night of their stay happened to coincide with the night of the Tiananmen Square protests in Beijing. Spread throughout our living room were not only a variety of Protestants and Catholics, but Muslims, Buddhists and Atheists including Communists. We all shared a meal while watching, riveted, to the events unfolding on the TV. A passage from the Bible was read aloud, in English and then in Chinese. The atmosphere was embracing, ecumenical, deeply human in our shared emotions.

Such gatherings were common in my parents' home. Indeed, my parents had been involved in ecumenical work from as far back as their student days. My parents are embracing of all Christian traditions, but much of the fundamentalist Protestant community of which our family was a part was decidedly antagonistic toward Catholic and Orthodox Christians, and even toward other Protestant denominations.

Growing up, I could not imagine that Catholics were bound for eternal damnation when they believed ninety percent or more of the same things as we did, but sometimes this was what I had been told. (Again, this was never by my parents, but by others in the evangelical community.) Rather than frighten me, this tempted me to know more about the Catholic Church. I developed a strong fascination with Catholicism, even though I hardly knew anything about it.

My parents owned and managed a Christian bookstore from before I was born until their retirement a few years ago. Through my teen years and into college, I worked in our family business, mostly on weekends or during summer and other school holidays. The customers were almost exclusively Protestant, and the merchandise reflected this. But there was one Catholic shelf in the back of the store. His decision to include this one shelf, my dad recently told me, caused him to take continual heat from the evangelical community. Some days I would be working the store alone. Seeing that the last customers had left, I would wander back to that shelf. Excitedly, I would open and read from a Catholic prayer book. A few times, after reading one of the prayers, I would cross myself cautiously, looking about to make sure no one had come into the store when I was not looking. It felt scandalous but exciting. I sensed a mystery of God that I had yet to discover.

I will not deny that, in large part, it was the vitriol so many of the evangelical Protestants who frequented the store had for Catholics that made me curious about Catholicism.

Even more so, it made me curious about *God*. I could not believe in a God who would shut his ear to people who worshiped him. God had to be bigger than any specific sect. My parents had taught me to believe in such a God, but I felt a disconnect with the fundamentalist Protestant community. And I knew I needed a community. That was why I sought out Catholicism. When I learned my ecumenical belief had a place within Catholicism, I knew I had found a home.

It was the acceptance of various forms of Christianity within Catholicism which drew me. The Catholic Church's ecumenism allowed me to accept it as an enhancement to the Christianity I already followed, rather than as a "conversion" from Protestantism.

This statement might shock people who cannot imagine the Catholic Church as an open-minded institution. And surely, the Catholic Church does not always behave as it is meant to. As I pointed out in the previous chapter, however, Catholicism's current, stated doctrine is one of acceptance, even if that is not always practiced. For me, that is significant.

The first time I attended a Catholic mass, during my senior year in college, I felt an immediate sense of belonging. During the general intercessions, a prayer was said for other Christian churches. It was not said with a mind to bring them to our way of thinking. It was prayed with pure, unambitious love. That prayer almost knocked me out of my seat. It was a complete turn from what I had experienced in fundamentalist Protestantism.

THE CHURCH'S SURPRISING POSITION

I have referred several times to the ecumenical language the Catholic Church used at the Second Vatican Council. It was then that it was first acknowledged there could be other ways for humanity to attain God. It is important to keep in mind just what the Church said, and, equally important, what it did *not* say. We will otherwise become confused by the objections to ecumenism voiced at the start of this chapter.

The Church indeed affirms God's ability to use the honest intentions toward goodness in any person, whether or not they know him within the Christian context. This is an act of God's grace—a love which seeks to find the beloved in any way possible. "Divine Providence does not deny the helps necessary for salvation to those who, without blame on their part, have not yet arrived at an explicit knowledge of God and with his grace strive to live a good life. Whatever good or truth is found amongst them is looked upon by the Church as a preparation for the Gospel."[22]

This is not a relativization of truth. This teaching maintains the primacy of Jesus as the figure of salvation and Catholicism as his Church. It does not lessen the responsibility of Catholics to live according to Christ's teaching. What it does is remove the cruelty of a judgment that is based on little more than family and cultural ties. It also, in all honesty, shields the Church from the judgment *it* would face from the many times when the Church has been a false witness to the gospel.

The potential for salvation is always through Jesus Christ, even for those who do not know Christ. Pope Benedict XVI called such seekers "Advent People," in that they are still awaiting the call of Christ.[23] In its way, the celebration of the season of Advent within Catholicism is for these, the people we affirm as our brothers and sisters, even if they do not yet know Christ

THE ESCHATOLOGICAL QUESTION

There is obviously a strong eschatological component to this question; it highlights, in my view, one of the major disconnects between Catholicism and fundamentalist Protestantism. How we view the after-life, and how it relates to this present life, is vastly different.

Simply put, fundamentalist Protestant after-life theology teaches that at the moment of death, the soul is transported either to heaven or hell, and that is that—for eternity. It is an instantaneous trip from the

---

[22] Vatican II: *Lumen Gentium*, 16

[23] Pope Benedict XVI: *Jesus of Nazareth*, Part Two, 7, 1

deathbed either to the throne of God or to the fires of hell. In Catholicism, the teaching is more nuanced. While purgatory is seldom taught outright anymore, a purgatorial essence is understood within the Catholic eschatological dialogue. Again in the former Pope's words, it is "an inwardly necessary process of transformation in which a person becomes capable of God."[24]

Thus, Catholics can safely speculate on an after-life where the soul still has room to grow. A person's incomplete journey toward God's truth can be used—through God's mercy—as the preparation for a journey that continues in the hereafter. Catholicism takes heaven and hell just as seriously as does Protestantism. The difference is that Catholic theology does not consider death a complete break between two lives. The Communion of Saints and prayers for the dead highlight the intertwined relationship between the two.

In fundamentalist Protestantism, by contrast, life on earth is seen as something of a rehearsal for the afterlife. The break between life and afterlife is the crucial moment. The key to entry into heaven is profession of faith in Jesus Christ. No amount of good works can replace this faith. The quest to convert the "lost," therefore, becomes an urgent and perilous task of mercy.

Fundamentalist Protestantism places inordinate weight on two specific moments: conversion by profession of faith, and death. In Catholicism, these processes are gradual. Conversion is not a moment, nor is the passage from life to after-life. Faith in Christ is not a profession. It is a lifestyle which must include

---

[24] J. Cardinal Ratzinger: *Eschatology,* 3, VII, 2, b

works of love to gain validation. This difference is the crux of the debate surrounding faith vs. works—*Sola Fide*—which has gone on since the first Apostles and was renewed with fervor during the Protestant Reformation. Protestantism places radical importance on the moments of profession of faith and earthly death.

For this reason, when a fundamentalist Protestant theologian speculates on a more nuanced after-life, his ideas are met with confrontation from the community. If death is not the defining moment, the entire structure of the eschatological theology begins to unravel. By postulating that salvation can be attained through a goodness apart from a profession of faith in Jesus Christ, or that that faith may still be achieved after death, the key element of Protestant conversion is broken down. Thus, those who do speculate on these questions usually do so in secret.

With this backdrop, it becomes clear why a constructive inter-religious dialogue cannot thrive within fundamentalist Protestantism. Its eschatological theology demands urgent evangelism. Though people often see the Protestant's evangelism as overbearing and judgmental, the actions come from a genuine spirit of love for those they see as *lost*.

Let me be clear that it is only the more extreme Protestant sects which consider the Catholic's stated faith in Jesus Christ as invalid. However, fundamentalist Protestantism cannot see the possibility for redemption in non-*Christian* religions without rendering some of its most basic tenets (specifically *Sola Fide*) irrelevant.

THE CHURCH OF TRADITION

Another point the Catholic Church emphatically maintains within its ecumenical literature is the tradition of the apostles, which is passed through an unbroken line to the leaders of the Church today.

This is the second major attribute of Catholicism that drew me. The rich history of wisdom and faith seems to be evidence of God's faithfulness over the Church. No institution or empire has ever lasted as long as has the Catholic Church. When so much corruption and wrong-doing has colored the Church's history, could it possibly have survived this long without God's protecting hand? Only God's grace can explain the Church's survival through the ages.

As a philosopher, this history is of the utmost importance to me. I actively lean on the Christian teachers of the past as a balance to my own questioning mind. I trust the wise Christian thinkers who have preceded me. I have married my own philosophical mind to this faith tradition. I can explore so many ideas upon the foundation that these men and women gave me. It is this philosophical tradition which builds the wall of Chesterton's playground, mentioned in chapter five. As discussed there, these walls are not a restriction to me; they are a liberation. I can safely throw myself into any philosophical challenge, trusting in the guiding embrace of the apostles and doctors of the Church.

This concept is anathema to modern philosophy. Some would call it naïvety. I call it humility.

Having faith that Christianity is true, I feel no need to start my philosophical inquiry from the very beginning, when so much work has already been accomplished. Further, why should I doubt the faith that has been gifted to me by the sacramental community of two thousand years? Only a foolish pride thinks to add more than the smallest morsel, either through thought or service, to such a vibrant tradition.

My choice to be Catholic springs from a desire to enjoin myself to this faith tradition—to nourish myself from the deposit of faith of all ages. By contrast, the very history of Protestantism, even the very word which is its name, makes me shy away. The issues afoot in the Reformation, over which Protestantism was born, were valid and severe. I would rather be part of the Church that in time absorbed the protests, considered them within the context of tradition, and eventually reformed, than the one that hastily broke off and took the word *Protest* for its name.

The Catholic Church certainly has flaws. It has never claimed not to. What it claims is to be Christ's flawed Church, tasked with carrying the Gospel through the ages.

It is this tradition, history, and perseverance that drew me to Catholicism on those lonely afternoons in my parents' bookstore. I am proud to now be a part of this history and eager to add my own faith to the deposit for future generations.

Despite common misperceptions, there is nothing restrictive or negative about this faith tradition. Rather, it is a tradition full of joy! It is also a tradition of love. It is a community not only of a local church, and not only of a global church, even. It is the community of a *historical* Church, with a communion of saints, a history of wisdom, and the guidance of the Holy Spirit to nourish it every day.

As I play in Chesterton's playground, I have identified the walls as doctrine and dogma—also known as *law*. But once we know them as *love*, they cease to feel like walls. The necessity of safe-keeping vanishes. Hans Urs von Balthasar wrote that: "outside of love, the law is nothing but a negative safeguard against the sin that is taken for granted."[25] So *with* love, the very law becomes a liberation. Christian faith is maintained by God's love, which is the backdrop to the ecumenism the world so desperately wants to accept.

Lord Jesus, through the intercession of the communion of saints, strengthen me with a steadfast and continual conversion to your will. Make me a vessel for the deposit of faith and an instrument of that same faith for years to come.

---

[25] Hans Urs von Balthasar: *Love Alone is Credible*, chap 7

MAKE IT MINE!

APPLYING THE LESSONS FROM THIS CHAPTER IN MY LIFE:

➤ Why do I believe what I do? Is it tradition or faith for me? Have I ever really made it mine?

➤ Think about how you came to be in your religion, whether it is Catholicism or another denomination. Is your religion a tradition that you received passively, or is it an active, purposeful choice?

➤ Make a list of moments in your past that have significantly affected your faith life and what you believe about God today. Pray for a new conversion, inspiring renewed passion for your faith.

PART III:
THE CHURCH IN THE MODERN WORLD

Nine: Vatican II And A Generation That Did Not Live Through It

"You are the light of the world. A city built on a hill cannot be hid. No one after lighting a lamp puts it under the bushel basket, but on the lampstand, and it gives light to all in the house. In the same way, let your light shine before others, so that they may see your good works and give glory to your Father in heaven." - Matthew 5:14-16

It is nearly impossible to address the current issues of Catholicism without reference to the Second Vatican Council of 1962-65. So much of what drives the discussion of today's Church draws on this legacy, with both progressive and conservative voices offering their perspectives on the council.

Having chosen Catholicism as an adult, I can say with certainty I would not be Catholic today were it not for this event. But I was born a decade and a half after Vatican II. I knew no "pre-conciliar Church." From my viewpoint, the council is a historical event. Its significance is clear to me, but I am not interested in the direction the Church intends to go after the council, as some still insist on discussing. The Church chose its direction after the council. We can now examine it through the eyes of history (how we can learn from it), rather than through the eyes of participation (how we will respond to it). Through that lens I look back on how the Church addressed the issues of the world five decades ago, not only learning and growing from the past, but also looking forward to the years ahead.

The Second Vatican Council provides the ideal beginning point for Part Three, which will examine some of the ways in which the Church seems to be out of touch with modernity as well as the proper Christian response to this perceived disconnect. Although I just stated my reticence to discuss the Church's response to the council, we must still discuss its aftermath, for, as an historical event, nothing else shaped the Church's direction in the twentieth century to such a strong degree.

The world has an unrealistic expectation of Christians. The council crystallized the Church's response to the world's expectations... meeting it here and now, with a truth valid through all time.

WHY WAS THE COUNCIL NEEDED?

The first half of the Twentieth Century was a stagnant period for Catholicism. The previous Church council (Vatican I) had, in many ways, set the Church in opposition to the world and set the clergy and religious within the Church apart from the laity. Intellectualism within the Church suffered. In 1907, Pope Pius X issued the encyclical *Pascendi Dominici Gregis*, renouncing "modernism" and establishing firm measures for controlling and censuring the clergy. [26] The strong threats issued by Pius X made the clergy

---

[26] Pope Pius X: *Pascendi Dominici Gregis*, 55

skittish to express modern thought on theological or social questions.

By the time of John XXIII's election as Pope in 1958, however, new ideas in the Church were becoming more difficult to silence. There was a clear need to make the liturgy more accessible to modern life. A wave of theological minds such as Karl Rahner and John Courtney Murray urged the Church to embrace a dose of modernism in order to keep it relevant. At the same time, others such as Hans Urs von Balthasar and Henri de Lubac advised a rediscovery of traditional Catholic teaching as a means of moving the Church forward in contrast to, but unashamedly *in,* the modern world.

Nobody expected much of Pope John XXIII. His election was regarded as a "transitional" selection. Indeed, he lived less than five years as pope. Yet in that short time, he had a greater influence on the Church than any other pope in the Twentieth Century.

In 1962, Pope John XXIII called together all the Cardinals and Bishops of the Church and launched the Second Vatican Council. He also invited scores of theologians, even ones who had been blacklisted by former Popes, such as John Courtney Murray. In short, Vatican II was called to reassess the Church's relationship to the world and the relationship of the clergy to the laity within the Church.

Some expected the Second Vatican Council to address specific social and moral questions. Instead, the council created a new framework with which to examine these questions. It avoided many specifics, however. Previously, the Church's focus had been on following moral rules. The Second Vatican Council put morality into a truly human context—it sought to convince people to follow morality because it is the right thing to do, not merely because the Church tells them to.

TIMELESS TRUTHS—NOT CURRENT ISSUES

Vatican II never intended to settle current social or theological issues. In the years since, however, both right and left have championed the council from their side of the debate. The dispute over which direction the council meant to take the Church has continued to this day. The modernist camp contends that the council left much unfinished. They even lament Pope John XXIII's mid-council death as a reason why certain controversial issues were not addressed.

Though many continue to argue how the council should have gone, or how it should now be interpreted, the event is past; its interpretation has been implemented. The lengthy papacy of John Paul II summarily concluded how the Church would interpret the council. It is no longer useful to argue over the meaning of the council. We should rather seek to study its lessons and implement them in our lives.

Those who contend that Popes John Paul II and Benedict XVI intended to take the Church back to a time before the council base their accusation upon a council which never occurred. That these Popes (to whom we may add Paul IV) have taken a strong stand against the modernist view on specific social issues, such as the rules of priesthood and the Church's sexual teachings, does not run counter to the spirit of the council, for the council did not directly explore these questions. Pope John Paul II devoted his entire papacy to obeying the actual texts of the council. Anyone who has read both the council documents and the writings of John Paul II, as well as the new catechism he commissioned, can hardly fail to see the former's influence upon the latter. It can be argued that no man has done more to advance the initiatives of Vatican II than John Paul.

Pope Benedict XVI's papacy did have some moments which were difficult to reconcile with the spirit of Vatican II. Yet when examining the complete corpus of Ratzinger's writings, the council's effect upon his thinking is clear. His emphasis on the Church's action within the world is dramatically influenced by the council's teachings.

WHAT DOES THE WORD "CATHOLIC" MEAN?

It betrays the intentions of the council to use it as rallying cry of progressive ideas. It equally betrays the spirit of the council not to allow such ideas to be heard. Pope John XXIII said at the onset of Vatican II that everything was on the table. The fact that some laws and traditions were left unchanged does not mean they were not addressed or prayed about. That same type of prayerful dialogue between progressive and conservative Catholic leaders is needed in our time.

The very word *catholic* as the adjective used to name our Church implies a diverse and varied collection of people. Merriam Webster's dictionary defines *catholic* as "universal; broad in sympathies, tastes or interests." The Roman Church adopted the word based on its use in the Nicene Creed, not the other way around.

Now think about the ways the Catholic Church is perceived today, both from outside the Church and from within. It is not a very *catholic* perception. Non-

Catholics have a perception that the Church is closed and intolerant. Within the Church, there are leading members with no tolerance for a difference of opinion. It is often suggested that Catholics who disagree with the Church leadership on social issues are not even real Catholics. This attitude goes against the spirit of the Second Vatican Council.

It is a sad fallacy to claim the word catholic yet deny the broadness in sympathies and tastes it implies. There is room within the Catholic Church for a variety of viewpoints. While some views are inevitably wrong, and maybe even heretical, God is big enough to have a relationship of love with all who worship him with a sincere heart.

The best example of a catholic group I can think of is Jesus' ragtag collection of followers. He traveled with rowdy fishermen, desert ruffians, war-mongers, prostitutes and cheating tax collectors. We don't know all the "hot-button" issues of their time, but of what we do know, there were bitter disputes over differences of opinion within the group. If Jesus assembled a similar group today, I can imagine there would be severe differences of opinion on our "hot-button" issues.

Accepting differences of opinion within the Catholic Church not only has the benefit of unity. It also has the benefit of creating honest dialogue surrounding the difficult issues of our time. Antagonism is never a successful stance from which to testify to the truth.

THE CHURCH AS THE LIGHT OF THE WORLD

The council set the Church up as a body that strives for the good of the whole world along with the salvation of the individual. Vatican II ended a separation in intent between the salvation of souls and the work of improving the dignity of human life. The Church now maintains the inseparability of these two purposes. "The Christian who shirks his duties toward his neighbor, neglects God himself and endangers his eternal salvation."[27] Salvation begins here and now. By improving human conditions through love, peace, charity and compassion, we are individually working toward our own salvation and communally demonstrating the example of Jesus through the Church's work in the world.

When I read the documents of Vatican II, I see a Church intent on making itself a body of love and acceptance in the world. It addresses the relationship of Church universal to clergy, parishes and laity, and lays out the proper way for the Church to meet the world. The dogmatic and theological questions that many of the priests of the time wished for the council to address remain unanswered. It is no longer useful to look to the council for those answers. The recent pontiffs have issued enough encyclicals to make the Church's positions clear. Therefore, we should take the council for what it was—a major step forward in the history of the Church's encounter with the world.

The fact that the world has undue expectations of the Church is not the Church's fault, but the world's. With the Second Vatican Council, the Church set itself up to be a light to the world (*Lumen Gentium*), not to conform to the world's wishes. Ratzinger, before becoming Pope, reminded us that: "it is not Christians who oppose the world, but rather the world which

---

[27] Vatican II: *Gaudium et Spes*, 43

opposes itself to them… The world waxes indignant when sin and grace are called by their names."[28]

There is still an ominous rift between modernists and traditionalists in the Church, but the dispute is mostly among those who lived through the council. Others, such as myself, who did not live through it, would not call ourselves modernist or traditionalist, progressive or orthodox, liberal or conservative. We are simply Catholics. We value the council for what it was and do not expect it to be something more. We love the tradition of the Church but also value new thoughts. We have rediscovered the teaching of the Church fathers, but are also fascinated by new ways of thinking about God and man. We are *post-conciliar* Christians.

The Church experienced some growing pains after the council, some of which continue today. But a generation of new Catholics stands ready to propel the Church forward. Vatican II gives valuable guidance in examining the questions of our time, but we have moved beyond the questions of half a century ago.

Once again, as discussed in Part One, today's Christian is confronted with a society that values freedom and tolerance above all else. The creed of the world is indeed a religion of freedom and a culture of tolerance. Vatican II helps shed light on how to meet this new philosophy. While the council documents clearly suggest a new tolerance for all, especially for those of other religions, it also defines freedom in a way at odds with the definition suggested by modern culture. The council identifies the "temptation to feel that our personal rights are fully maintained only when

---

[28] Vittorio Messori: *The Ratzinger Report*, chap. 2

we are exempt from every restriction of divine law. But this is the way leading to the extinction of human dignity, not its preservation."[29] It is only within the context of law that freedom has meaning.

The Second Vatican Council opened the Church up to the world, but this opening cannot be misconstrued as a lifting of the Church's law. This has been repeatedly affirmed by the leaders of the Church since the council, from Paul VI to John Paul II to Benedict XVI and clearly now to Pope Francis.

"The Church, 'like a stranger in a foreign land, presses forward amid the persecutions of the world and the consolations of God,'[30] announcing the cross and death of the Lord until he comes (I Corin. 11:26). But by the power of the risen Lord she is given strength to overcome, in patience and in love, her sorrows and her difficulties, both those that are from within and those that are from without, so that she may reveal in the world, faithfully, however darkly, the mystery of her Lord until, in the consummation, it shall be manifested in full light."[31]

Lord Jesus, protect and bless your pilgrim Church, and keep it faithful to your teachings. Let it never forget its mission and calling to shine as a light in the world.

---

[29] *Gaudium et Spes,* 41

[30] St. Augustine: *De Civitate Dei,* XVIII, 51, 2

[31] Vatican II: *Lumen Gentium,* 8

MAKE IT MINE!

APPLYING THE LESSONS FROM THIS CHAPTER IN MY LIFE:

➢ Does my assurance in my own views and positions ever make me arrogant?

➢ Think about what the word "catholic" means to you. What do you think of first when you hear the word? Does the definition given above change your perception of the Catholic Church in any way?

➢ Consider taking the time to read some of the documents of Vatican II. They are easily available on the Vatican website. *Lumen Gentium* and *Gaudium et Spes* are good ones to start with. You may be amazed by what you learn about the Church and its stated mission in the world.

Ten: The Role Of The Clergy

"For it is fitting that we should have such a high priest, holy, blameless, undefiled, separated from sinners, and exalted above the heavens. For the law appoints as high priests those who are subject to weakness, but the word... appoints a Son who has been made perfect forever." - Hebrews 7:26,28

While the Second Vatican Council helped the Church become more relevant in current society, the Church is still placed at odds with the modern world in many ways. Because of the precedent set by Vatican II, many people, both from outside and within the Church, continue to challenge it to become more in step with modern ways. Perhaps the primary place where this can be seen is in the role of the priest.

To put it bluntly, the idea of celibacy is bizarre to the modern conscience. Likewise, the authority and masculinity of the position is unacceptable to modern values. There are deeper complexities to these questions which the Church has been wise to consider.

SUBMISSION TO AUTHORITY

The authority of the Catholic priestly hierarchy is problematic to many modern-minded Catholics. Does God really intend for us to submit to the authority of men who are often corrupt, selfish, or simply flawed despite the good intentions of their hearts?

From a historical perspective, does such a structure even fit with what Jesus intended for his Church? It would be helpful to examine how this structure came into place.

As the original disciples aged and began to die, Christians found it necessary to establish some semblance of authority. With such a rapidly expanding religion, it would be naïve to expect that it could function without figures of authority. By the second century, the offices of bishop and priest had been formally established. Despite the flaws in this system, the Church has continued to call lay people to adhere to this authority.

True Christianity maintains the equality of all human beings, men and women, slave and free, and regardless of race. Yet interestingly, Christianity discourages the individual from fighting for one's own equality if it means going against established authority. We are obligated to fight for equality when we see injustice toward others. But if *I* am being treated with inequality, I am called to accept it and unite my suffering with the suffering and inequality borne by Jesus. This idea is anathema to post-Enlightenment thinking, but it is the truth of Jesus' teachings. He forbade the nation of Israel from fighting for its freedom from Rome. Likewise, Paul sends the slave Onesimus back to his master Philemon.

As Christian lay people, we are therefore obligated to accept and respect the authority of the priest, bishop, and Pope. Perhaps this authority is not ideal; after all, they are sinners no less than we. Still, these men have given their imperfect lives over to the service of God. By submitting to their authority, we certainly have it better than the Israelites, who had to give themselves over to Caesar, or Onesimus, who had to return to slavery!

Christianity is not an Enlightenment religion, nor is it a religion that teaches freedom. It teaches service. While we should strive for the freedom of others, standing up to oppression, we can never be so tied to our own freedom that we compromise higher virtues.

PATRIARCHAL UNDERPINNINGS

In addition to the authority of the priesthood, its masculinity runs counter to the values of the modern world. This presents a problem for those who would like to see the Church open the priesthood to women.

The history of Christianity has risen through male-dominant cultures. Though Jesus had female followers throughout his ministry, when he was preparing to leave the world, he laid the duty of authority for continuing his ministry upon the eleven male disciples. Due to the patriarchy of Jewish, Greek, and Roman culture, the Church's early authority continued to be held exclusively by men. As Christianity moved from its Middle Eastern heritage, it became primarily a European religion, with seats of power in both Rome and Constantinople. Europe, of course, was just as patriarchal as had been the earlier seats of Christendom. The question of allowing women in the priesthood never arose.

Considering the cultures which have promulgated Christianity, it is obvious why the authority was held by men.

We live in a new era. Europe and America are in every way post-Enlightenment cultures. Equality is rightfully prioritized in society. Women are accepted in positions of authority. Though, in many ways,

Enlightenment thinking has had an adverse impact on world thought from the Christian perspective, this is one area where the Church might be able to learn from it.

When it came to equality, particularly the equality of the sexes, Jesus was himself an Enlightenment thinker. Despite the patriarchy of the time, Jesus had a revolutionary attitude toward women, including them in his close circle of trusted companions. Forcing women into lesser roles, both in society and the Church, runs counter to the teachings of Jesus.

Having a greater role for women within the Church is not only a matter of equality. The Church would benefit from a greater female influence, giving it a more balanced, wholly human perspective.

When Jesus was teaching at the home of Mary and Martha, Mary sat at his feet learning. Her sister Martha tried to call her away to complete her role as hostess. Martha essentially implied that the teachings of spirituality should be left to the men while the women served them. But Jesus said: *"Mary has chosen the better part, which will not be taken away from her."* (Luke 10:42). Jesus was not condemning Martha's efforts of service, but he vigorously condemned the claim that spiritual participation and the learning of scripture were restricted to men. Mary is afforded the same place in the spiritual company of Jesus as his male disciples. Yet like Martha, women in Christianity have been given the servant's role while the men maintain their authority and priestly order alone.

Therefore, in the greater post-Enlightenment world of Europe and North America, it would seem the time has come to at least examine the question of allowing women in the priesthood—to allow this question to be discussed in open and prayerful dialogue.

However, the demographics of Catholicism have changed. Its culture is still very European, but it is no longer a European religion. In the last century, as European enthusiasm for the religion has dwindled, Catholicism has spread like wildfire in the Southern Hemisphere. Presently, there are more practicing Catholics in South and Central America, Africa and South Asia than in North America and Europe.

Much of the reason for this shift is that the southern half of the world has been less affected by the Enlightenment and the ensuing materialism which made Christianity seem irrelevant. For that very reason, the authority of a female priest in many of those cultures would be more difficult to accept. If the Church allowed women to be priests and sent them to the developing world as the symbol of Catholic authority, they may not garner the same respect as would men. In Europe and the United States, we tend to think the world revolves around us. In our cultures, female priests would represent a marvelous advance of equality (not to mention a cure for the priest shortage!). The Magesterium prudently considers the impact this change would have in the places where Catholicism is currently strongest.

Perhaps the day will come when the Church seriously considers welcoming women into the priesthood, but at present I understand its reticence.

THE RESPONSIBILITIES OF SEXUALITY

The other aspect of Catholic priesthood which runs directly counter to post-Enlightenment thinking is celibacy.

The historical argument is often brought against requiring celibacy of the priesthood. It is probable that many of the early apostles had wives; we know Peter had a wife. Yet as early as Paul, sexual continence was encouraged of the teachers of the gospel. The detractors of priestly celibacy point to the two Lateran Councils of the Twelfth Century, which for the first time stringently enforced celibacy in the priesthood. Celibacy had been strongly recommended of the priesthood in Church council documents dating as early as the Fourth Century. It took almost eight hundred years for Church leadership to realize that "strong encouragement" was not sufficient. Celibacy had to be enforced and its failure punished.

Is this an archaic rule, or does it still have value in our time? Our culture certainly finds it archaic. Many within the Catholic Church agree.

In order to understand why the Church places such importance on maintaining a celibate clergy, it is first necessary to examine the meaning of sex and its place in our culture.

With so much of our culture focused on sex, we are now conditioned to believe that sex is one of the most natural functions of the body. Any limit placed on our full sexual expression is frowned upon.

Sex is a beautiful gift God gave us in his design of creation. It also comes with a responsibility that the proponents of sexual liberation would rather escape. If we are to speak of sex as a natural function of the body, and the desire for it as something equally natural, then it is important to remember its full functionality, which includes not only the production of new human life, but also the bond of two people which is achieved in no other way. So while God did indeed give us sex as a beautiful and pleasurable gift, he also ordained that it lead toward reproduction, and that it unite two people in a strong bond of love.

Through the development of various contraceptive methods, contemporary society has decoupled much of sex's connection with procreation. People can now have sex with relative confidence that no pregnancy will occur. The ensuing debates over the moral implications of contraception have caused both secular society and the Church to lose track of the other function God gave to the sexual act—the bond between two people.

As sex has become easier and fewer children have resulted, society has come to consider it normal to have far more than one sexual partner in a lifetime. This is unnatural. The act of sex creates a bond which can only be broken with great pain. Our culture actually encourages people to have a multiplicity of sexual partners, ignoring the now commonplace pain of severing a sexual relationship. God intended this bond to be inseparable—hence the sacrament and *vocation* of marriage. Sex is intended to create an unbreakable bond and a responsibility between two people.

Much has been made of the Catholic Church's opposition to contraception, but contraception is not really the issue. The Church's true opposition is toward the loose sexuality that causes people so much emotional pain. Contraception has simply made sex so easy that we often fail to consider the consequences. Contraception is not the issue. Casual promiscuity is the issue. The Church makes clear that its opposition to contraception is out of a fear that it will open the door for infidelity, promiscuity, and a general disrespect for the union of two hearts created in the sexual act.

In one of the most controversial encyclicals ever written, *Humanæ Vitæ*, Pope Paul VI implored us to "consider how easily this course of action could open wide the way for marital infidelity and a general lowering of moral standards. Not much experience is needed to be fully aware of the human weakness and to understand that human beings—and especially the young, who are so exposed to temptation—need incentives to keep the moral law, and it is an evil thing to make it easy for them to break that law."[32] It goes on to point out the effect that such disrespect for the natural consequences of sex can have on the emotional well-being of the people involved.

FOCUSED VOCATION

It may seem that we have diverged from the topic of the priesthood, but it is necessary to understand the consequences of sex before seeing the true good of celibacy.

Sex leads to bonds, and bonds create true family. When a man and woman engage in the act of sex, even if no children result, they have created a bond, whether or not they consummate it publicly with the sacrament of marriage. These people are thereafter called to care for one another. Human nature compels them to do so. The Church only demands they follow what nature dictates.

Therefore, if a priest intends to devote himself fully to the will and service of God (and likewise a monk or a nun), he must free himself from the commitment intrinsic in the sexual act. This is why the Church calls marriage a vocation, just as priesthood is a vocation. In

---

[32] Pope Paul VI: *Humanæ Vitæ*, 17

marriage, one serves God through love for another human being. In priesthood, one serves God through service to the faithful. If a priest also had a family, his duty would be split, and when he had problems in his family life, he would need to devote himself to that, taking away from his duty to the faithful. One need only look at a small cross-section of Protestant ministers to see how true this can be.

The priest has a duty to serve his congregation. That is the family God has given him. In our culture, it is difficult to understand how one could renounce sex for the entirety of his life. This is a great sacrifice, but the Church maintains its necessity for the priest to be fully committed to the duty he has undertaken. If priests were allowed to marry, the ensuing complications would be great. Could their spouses be content to be second to the congregation in the priest's life? *Should* the spouse be second to his work? What would happen if the marriage failed? Would the priest want to remarry?

For all the scandals the priesthood has faced in recent decades, it would only increase if total celibacy were no longer demanded. For single priests, the temptation to fornicate would be extreme. For priests with families, life would be precariously demanding.

Celibacy removes the distraction of sex from the life of the priest.

St. Augustine pointed out that total abstinence is easier than perfect moderation. [33] Thus the Church continues to demand total celibacy and is wise to do so.

Renouncing a physical pleasure such as sex is not considered natural by our "enlightened" age; it

---

[33] St. Augustine: *De Bono Conjugali,* 25

considers the vocation to celibate life a burden. But this is not necessarily so. Many find it to be a relief, and others an absolute joy. If you assume it is a burden, I encourage you to speak with priests, monks and nuns who have taken this vow, and you may be surprised what you hear. Every priest I have known well absolutely loved their life and their work. They were some of the happiest, most fulfilled people I have met.

If it was such a burden, we would see a much greater number turn away from their vocation at some point in their lives, but this is very rare. More likely, they echo the joy expressed by St. Thérèse of Lisieux upon entering the Carmelite order. "This happiness was not passing," she affirmed. "It did not take its flight with the illusions of the first days. Illusions, God gave me the grace not to have a single one when entering Carmel. With what deep joy I repeated those words: 'I am here forever and ever!'"[34]

Taking the vows of priesthood is a sacrifice which requires a great deal of courage, but as St. Thérèse expressed, and as so many have discovered, the rewards are surpassingly worthwhile.

My soul magnifies you, oh Lord, and my spirit rejoices in God my savior. (Luke 1:46-47) You have honored me to do your work and blessed me to call myself your servant!

---

[34] St. Thérèse of Lisieux: *Story of a Soul,* chap 7

MAKE IT MINE!

APPLYING THE LESSONS FROM THIS CHAPTER IN MY LIFE:

➢ What is my vocation? How seriously do I take it?

➢ Every Christian has a vocation. It is part of the call to follow Christ. Pray for the discernment to know what your true vocation is, and then for strength and courage to follow it.

➢ Pope Benedict XVI called vocation "the fruit of an intimate dialogue between the Lord and his disciples."[35] You are a disciple. In what specific ways is the fruit of your dialogue with God visible to the world?

---

35 Pope Benedict XVI: Response to the Questions of the American Bishops, 3. April 16, 2008

Eleven: The Work Of Social Justice

"My child, do not keep needy eyes waiting. Do not grieve the hungry, or anger one in need. Do not add to the troubles of the desperate, or delay giving to the needy. Do not reject a suppliant in distress, or turn your face away from the poor…" - Sirach 4:1-4

For religion to be relevant in the world, it cannot simply stand on the sidelines of world events. It must be willing to take a stand for the truth.

Certain religions and even certain Christian sects advocate separation from the world as the path to holiness. As Catholics, our religion demands involvement in the work of social justice and human dignity. This is missionary work which carries weight. St. James says to *"be doers of the word, and not merely hearers."* (James 1:22) And again, *"I by my works will show you my faith."* (James 2:18) Without loving action to go along with our belief, Christianity is little more than a collection of nice ideas.

This was one of the primary points of the Second Vatican Council. Catholic teaching speaks of "taking part in salvation history," meaning that through the practice of our religion, we actively work to bring humanity toward the fulfillment of God's kingdom.

MADE IN THE IMAGE OF GOD

The Judeo-Christian belief that humanity is made in the image of God gives the human person an individual dignity and glory beyond anything that could be otherwise conceived. Each and every human person actively bears the image of God.

Other spiritualities seek either to exalt the natural world or to unite the human consciousness to nature. But Christians know that we are higher than the natural world... that we are different from the animals. We hold a special place in reality. Indeed, we know that the entire natural world was made as a gift from God to us. All things on earth are related to the human individual "as their center and crown."[36] It is with no hesitation that the Christian thus exalts the human individual, for it does so within the context of God's loving gift.

Despite this great gift of glory and dignity, humanity has rebelled throughout history against our identity as the image of God. This stems from our aversion to authority. We would rather rely on ourselves and exalt humanity. As soon as we attempt to gain exaltation free from God, we wind up breaking down our own dignity.

History is rife with examples of this: from the Tower of Babel to today's spiritualization of science, in which the human individual, in attempting to glorify himself, reduces himself to nature's equal. Francis Schaeffer laments humanity's tragedy from the Age of Enlightenment onward: "Man beginning with his proud, proud humanism, tried to make himself autonomous, but rather than becoming great, he had

---

[36] Vatican II: *Gaudium et Spes*, 12

found himself ending up as only a collection of molecules—and nothing more."[37]

The human individual can only realize his glory and dignity as the image of God. Any other attempt at exaltation reduces him to the level of the nature over which he should be master.

Building on the knowledge that all men and women are made in the image of God, The Catholic Church maintains the rights to this glory and dignity in each and every person. Pope John Paul II said that the defense of this basic dignity has been entrusted to us by God, and that it is the responsibility of the men and women of every age.[38]

The Second Vatican Council, which so stressed this topic, declared it the individual Christian's "inescapable duty to make ourselves the neighbor of every man, no matter who he is, and if we meet him, to come to his aid in a positive way."[39] Everyone has the right to life and basic means for dignified living. In the story of the rich man and Lazarus, from the sixteenth chapter of Luke, the rich man is condemned not only for his greed, but because he denied Lazarus the ability to achieve the basic dignity which was his right.[40]

A CALL TO PEACE AND EQUALITY

If every person is made in the image of God, then the equality of all human persons is a goal which must be actively pursued. There is no room for racism, sexism, or discrimination of any kind.

---

[37] F. Schaeffer: *How Should we then Live*, chap 8

[38] Pope John Paul II: *Sollicitudo rei Socialis*, 47

[39] *Gaudium et Spes*, 27

[40] ibid

Unfortunately, Christian history has a poor track record when it comes to human equality. In the relationship between nations, between races, and between sexes, the Church has been among the worst offenders.

Dozens of wars have been waged under the blasphemous banner of Christ. If everyone is equally made in the image of God, any act of violence, either by nations or by individuals, is an affront to that holy image. Every time God's image is soiled with blood, it reduces humanity's dignity.

Western society has made much progress in the effort toward human equality in the past centuries and particularly in recent decades. The Church too, especially in the half century since Vatican II, has made a great deal of progress. Yet in many ways, racism, sexism, and geopolitical strife have simply changed shape, not been eliminated. It is imperative that we examine these problems in a fresh light, not with an eye toward the past.

Fighting for justice and equality is very different from fighting for individual freedoms—something I have been speaking against throughout this book. Our society often confuses equality with freedom, thus missing the true meaning of both.

THE ACTIVE CONSEQUENCE OF BEARING GOD'S IMAGE

If it is true that we are created in God's image and that Jesus is the living incarnation of God on earth, loving us enough to bear our suffering on the cross, then that truth carries a consequence. Jesus charged us to follow his commandments and example. This charge is exactly what the knowledge that we are made in

God's image should compel us to do. Simply put, it is to love your neighbor as yourself. (Luke 10:27)

If we believe that we were made in God's image, the logical result is an obligation toward loving kindness.

If the most marginalized human being was made in the image of God, then I must help that person in their time of need. If I fail this obligation, then Christ may rightly say to me, *"I was hungry and you gave me no food, I was thirsty and you gave me nothing to drink, I was a stranger and you did not welcome me, naked and you did not give me clothing, sick and in prison and you did not visit me."* (Matt. 25:42-43) What presumption, not to aid one who bears the image of God!

It is for the good of all that we bear each other up. I should never meet another person and forget that he or she is made in the image of God. If one person bears God's image, then all people must bear God's image. We are all equal in this, and none has an advantage over others.

Sometimes it is difficult to see God's image in certain individuals. Jesus' teaching compels us to find it, and to recognize the good in even the most unlovely of persons. The question bears asking: If certain people do not seem to reflect the divine image, I must consider whether it may be difficult for others to see God's image in *me*. If so, then how willing will they be to offer compassion in *my* time of need? Love must be given to all, no matter how difficult some people are to love or how much my self-righteousness tries to separate me from them.

Jesus' commandment of doing good toward our neighbor comes from a call to love.

Catholic teaching lays an additional responsibility upon us by making this call out of justice as well. It is *just* that all humans be given their basic rights and dignity. Love is the higher calling, of course, but when we do not have the strength and true compassion to reach a place of love, we are still called to act out of justice.

Social justice is an ongoing task for the human family. The Christian is called urgently to mitigate the suffering caused by poverty, malnutrition, disaster, and disease. Helping those in need is not optional for Christians. The turning of a blind eye is an eye turned away from God.

INSEPARABILITY OF LOVE AND CHRISTIANITY

Love is the key to living as a Christian. Following Jesus' teachings and example requires me to love others to my maximum ability. This love takes the form of charity.

Charity is often defined simplistically as giving money to the poor, but this misses the essence of its meaning. Charity is an act of sharing from the abundance of God's gifts. It is an act of spontaneous goodness. Charity is the most intimate activation of social justice. If I perceive that another person is in need, charity obliges that I come to that person's aid in the knowledge that God's abundance can take care of my needs as well. Charity places those who have plenty in solidarity with the poor and allows both to enjoy the blessing of God's abundance.

Jesus told us to give to anyone who asked of us and to treat others as we would wish for them to treat us. Thus, the Catholic Church has, throughout its history, defined charity as its primary purpose and goal.

Pope Francis uses a beautiful metaphor in calling the Church a field hospital after a battle.

It can be argued that charity is the duty of all religions. The Dalai Lama rightly described religion as the medicine which cures human suffering.[41] It is the accountability that religion gives its practitioners that spur them to bring this medicine, in the form of love, to the poor and marginalized of the world.

Love is a labor without end. The more I learn to act with love, the more need for it I discover. Sometimes, the world's despair and the rifts in humanity, seem too much to heal by one individual's act of love, but they are not too much. No offer of love is too small. Love is contagious. The first act of love can spread like a flame that begins with one match but can set a whole forest ablaze. The forest is hatred and injustice. The fire is love. The match is one single person.

The power of love which God placed in each of us can indeed change the world!

Lord God, give me the courage to work for justice and dignity in the world. Use my small works of goodness as the first sparks to light a great fire of love. Let me never be afraid to change the world!

---

[41] The Dalai Lama: *Spiritual Advice for Buddhists & Christians*, chap 1

MAKE IT MINE!

APPLYING THE LESSONS FROM THIS CHAPTER IN MY LIFE:

➢ Do I fully believe in the promise of being made in God's image? Am I worthy of this distinction?

➢ Pray for the ability to consistently recognize God's image in others, especially those in whom it is difficult to see.

➢ When you encounter people (either friends or strangers) who are difficult to love, call to mind the lesson of Matthew 25:42-43. Think of that person really being Christ. Then act accordingly. Recognize how your behavior changes.

Twelve: Charity In The Age Of Labor

"'Lord, when was it that we saw you hungry or thirsty or a stranger or naked or sick or in prison, and did not take care of you?' Then he will answer them, 'Truly I tell you, just as you did not do it to one of the least of these, you did not do it to me.'" - Matthew 25:44-45

A byproduct of modern society's glorification of *freedom* is a feeling of independence, whereby one individual does not think they need anyone else. This humanistic claim is rooted in the rejection of gratitude for the good gifts of the earth. After all, without a loving God, *we* would be the ones to credit for the beauty and goodness that surrounds us. It is hailed as a testament both to human ingenuity and the perseverance of our noble single-celled ancestors. Through our knowledge, work and tenacity we are told that we have accomplished everything on our own.

This perspective is not only self-centered, it is tragically ignorant. In the end, it can only lead to despair. It cuts us off not only from God's love, but ultimately from the love of our neighbors as well. We saw earlier how important a sense of community is to our happiness. Unselfish care and compassion build community and thus give life its joy. Jesus did not prescribe his social program merely as an order or even as a path toward salvation. By acting with love in

125

society, we fill ourselves and those around us with joy, making life abundantly more worthwhile.

THE VIRTUE OF WORK

This feeling of social independence—of feeling that we need nobody besides ourselves—is relatively new to human history. To a large degree, it stems from a changing view on labor in society. The concept and value associated with work has changed a great deal over time, particularly since the Industrial Revolution. Work is now seen as a virtue. For some of us, work has virtually become our god. But that was not always the way.

How did this new perspective of work come about? And, more importantly for our discussion, how does it fit with Christian beliefs and specifically Jesus' teachings concerning the poor and underprivileged?

The developed world has come away from the class model of past centuries into an age of labor. No longer does a person born in poverty necessarily face an entire life in that state. The poor have the hope of rising to a higher social level. That hope is far from certain, but it is more realistic than in previous ages. Immigration to the Americas has been a big part of this process. Usually those who immigrate in poverty fail to climb out of it in their lives, but through hard work and education, their children can achieve a better life. The common theme is work. We believe that despite any hardship, through work humans can rise from one class to another.

Even in light of the economic crisis in the United States and Europe, and with the rampant unemployment that followed, our core beliefs have not changed. Policy makers immediately identified job creation as the most important step toward climbing out of the economic hole. The disparity of wages between the top and bottom of the income spectrum is one of the main causes of the crisis. Recognition of these factors comes from our belief in the virtue of work and fair wages.

We take the value of labor for granted now, but it is completely foreign to the model of the middle ages and the ancient world. Then, work was considered a hardship. If you had to work, you were looked down on by those lucky enough not to. Conversely, the workers revered the rich—lazy and fruitless as their lives may have been.

The rise of the merchant class began to make work more of a fair exchange. So did the manufacturing boom of the late nineteenth century, which suddenly required huge amounts of human labor. For many years, manufacturing labor was only a small step ahead of slavery, but the difference was hope. Over time, the middle class became a dominant economic force. No longer do the many labor for the comfort of the few.

Work has now become one of our most admired virtues, and for good reason. By working, we propel forward the entire human race. In the past, the working class ran the machine that supported the lives of both rich and poor. Now all are expected to pitch in and run the machine of society. It is an amazing act of teamwork and unity. Think of how many people are affected by the work you do. And when you sit in the comfort of your home, think of how many people's labor supports you right then: the builder of your house, the electrician who wired it, those who run your water and sewer, those who supplied the food for your last meal—the list could go on and on. Every worker in the world is connected in this great dance. We do not work for wages so much; we work so the human machine may continue. Wages are merely the means through which our work and the work of others are coordinated. Understanding this interdependence immediately breaks down the foolish notion of individuality that often comes in the wake of success.

Work is indeed a virtue, but it is a social virtue, not something private. It is one of the ways we experience community.

Work is an act of love. In your effort to provide a service to another, you are giving a gift of your talent, and in paying another for their labor, you in turn accept their gift of talent. It is an exchange of love, which we all too often disguise as an exchange of greed. With your work you act in love toward those who, with you, spend their days in labor, and they at the same time act with love toward you.

Even when we complain about our work, we intrinsically know this principal. If we live in fair-labor societies, we are thankful for our work, especially as so many struggle with unemployment. We recognize the loving trade that is work and are thankful to live in a time and place where this exchange is allowed.

But where has this left the world's poor?

IS CHARITY STILL VALID?

This age of labor has given more people the opportunity to step into the human machine and realize dreams and ambitions through work. It has also equipped many of us with a "high horse." We ignore the suffering of those around us with a clear conscience.

Work itself is an act of love, but we cannot ignore the other forms love takes or our obligation to ease suffering by sharing the beauty that was so freely given to us.

The primary thrust of Jesus' social program was care for the poor. He advocated charity and compassion from the beginning to the end of his ministry. Do the specifics of his teachings still apply? After all, he lived in a different era. It was not a fair-labor society by any stretch of the imagination. Jesus lived in a time of polarized economic classes and strong nationalistic prejudices. So we tend to separate ourselves, saying the poor do not need our charity, but rather the justice of consequence and the opportunity to rise.

Our elevation of the virtue of work has devalued the virtue of charity in our society. In this age, it has become tempting to pass judgment on the poor. The beggar in the plaza is viewed as lazy. Why doesn't he go get a job? We are tempted to pass judgment on him before we seek to know anything about him. The other side of this is that many of the recently unemployed—victims of the economic crisis or squeezed out by technology and outsourcing—are ashamed to ask for help, even from their families and friends.

Pope Benedict XVI wrote about this concept in his encyclical, *Deus Caritas Est:* specifically about the relationship between capital and labor in society. Now that labor is the primary means of capital, we are reluctant to give capital (alms) except as payment for labor. [42] Thus charity is now often disregarded as a thing of the past.

---

[42] Pope Benedict XVI: *Deus Caritas Est,* 26

We think we only gained what we have through our own effort and abilities, and we look down on those who don't work as hard. Perhaps we will send some money to a third-world country to satisfy our conscience, but it is a different matter entirely to help the poor in our own city! We are reluctant to support a career of laziness. With the fall of the class system and the rise of greater social programs, affluent people have lost their feeling of obligation to help those in need. Those who do practice charity are considered (both by themselves and others) as altruistic rather than fulfilling their duty.

We can look at the charitable workers of history from a safe distance, pointing out that in those times social class determined wealth and poverty. Of course it was virtuous for the wealthy to give to the poor, because the wealthy did nothing to deserve their wealth, nor the poor their poverty. Now days, by contrast, wealth is associated with work, while poverty is associated with laziness. Few would admit feeling this way when put so bluntly, but the prejudice has been deeply rooted in the collective western consciousness for several generations.

WORK IS OUR PRIVILEGE—NOT OUR RIGHT

You may argue that it is often true! Many of the poor and homeless we encounter really are lazy, or are only begging to support a lifestyle of addiction. Perhaps you are right. But when did Jesus ever tell us to be compassionate toward those who deserved compassion? He never said "give to those who need it," but "give to those who *ask*." Jesus makes no distinction in his call to charity. The same commandment is given to the rich man as to the slave.

The former is called to sell all he has and give to the poor (Matt. 19:21). The latter is told to work hard for his master. (Luke 12:43). These are hardly values our contemporary culture would embrace, but they were no less difficult to swallow in Jesus' time. His message is as pertinent in today's age of labor as when he first gave it.

How can we know what led the beggar we ignore to his position? And, whatever the causes, who are we to judge? It is a fine line that separates us from him.

There is a gross fallacy in the claim that our affluence was earned by our work—the sweat of our proverbial brow. It is the gift of those who came before us, pioneering this age of labor to give us the right to work for our own gain. In past centuries, unless you were one of the privileged few, you would have worked your whole life and never accumulated any savings or comfort. So next time you feel so accomplished for the strides you have made in business, consider those who preceded you by a few generations. Think of their toil and the gift it was to you. As hard as you may work, they undoubtedly worked harder, in less comfort, only for the hope that their descendants would have a better life. Make them proud by honoring their gift.

It is selfish and arrogant to claim success as entirely one's own. Could any of us have lived and worked as our own ancestors did, providing such profound change for future generations? Their work is our gift. Our charity is our gratitude.

How can we presume to think that we deserve the gifts we have been given? Do I, born in the excessively affluent United States, deserve the right to work for wealth and comfort more than one born in a country without these freedoms and this affluence? Do I even deserve my sobriety more than the man addicted to drugs or alcohol? How close could any of us be to him, or he to any of us, given the same opportunities? How many degrees of separation really exist between us?

While work is one of our greatest acts of love and the means by which we enter the communal effort of humanity, it is no excuse to ignore our duty to the poor. Jesus' commandments regarding the poor are just as valid today as ever. Our work is a gift to humanity, but our ability to work is a gift to us. We have no right to claim it as our own.

Pope John Paul II defined charity as "the work of human solidarity." [43] We have a responsibility of compassion for everyone who shares the image of God. Our compassion must be ready at a moment's notice, whenever it is called for, just as we would hope for others to give it in our own time of need.

THE VOCATION OF LOVE

When work and charity are kept in balance and both retain their purpose of communal love, they take on a salvific character. Whatever form our work takes, the purpose of our work, both physical and spiritual, is love and solidarity with our community. Both work and charity bring us closer to the fulfillment of our innermost desires—the peace of true love.

The highest work is not that which we call our career. The highest form of work comes in the form of virtue, which springs from the love of one person for the community of the world. Virtue is achieved when the good of the whole is put ahead of the will of the one. If we distract ourselves with too many selfish

---

[43] Pope John Paul II: *Salvifici Doloris*, 29

pursuits, we forget how to act with virtue. Or worse—
we choose to ignore virtue, for it is seldom easy and
never convenient. Virtue calls us to abandon our own
comfort for another's need. There is a sacrifice that
comes from the knowledge that we are made in the
image of God. It is that virtue must take precedence
over rest, charity over comfort. Those who need your
virtue and your charity just as surely reflect the image
of God as do you.

Always work in a spirit of communal love. Do not
work to separate yourself from others through wealth
and status, but work to stand in unity with them. If you
just work to hoard wealth, your only reward will be
stress. Such accumulation only leads to increased desire
for things. Rather, work so that the goodness of your
labor will benefit the world and those you love. What
other reward can really be attained, and how will you
get there? The higher the ambition, the more fickle are
the forces that hold it in place. The greater the gain of
wealth, power or fame, the more perilous, and indeed
imminent, is the fall. If, however, you turn your
ambition toward love, you will find that you have
already achieved your goal. This is true contentment,
such that wealth and possessions can never bring.

When a rich young man asked Jesus how he could
gain eternal life (Matt. 19: 21-22), Jesus told him to sell
all his possessions and give the money to the poor.
Rather than obeying, the young man went away
grieving. Why did this young man hold so tightly to the
very thing that gave him grief? Jesus told him how to
be free from grief, but the man valued the comfort of
his possessions more than the true comfort that would
have come through a life of charity and love.

The person whose contentment and identity is wrapped up in their selfish work has no time for the virtuous life Jesus offered the man in Matthew's gospel. The tragedy for this person is that their selfish labor gives no contentment—not at present, nor in the future. The young man in the gospel went away *grieving!* What kind of satisfaction in wealth and possessions is this?

Lord God, instill me with a spirit of charitable Christian love. Open my eyes to the needs of those you have put in my life, in all the subtle ways those needs manifest themselves. Let the value of my work never keep me from standing in solidarity with the poor, underprivileged and oppressed.

MAKE IT MINE!

APPLYING THE LESSONS FROM THIS CHAPTER IN MY LIFE:

- ➤ How much of my identity is tied to my work? Has the modern valuation of work ever caused me to judge others?
- ➤ Try to imagine Jesus present in our society and our time. How would his teachings change? Would they change at all? What kind of people would he gather as disciples?
- ➤ Make a conscious effort to separate the virtue of work from charitable Christian love in your own life. Find tangible and creative ways to help or be in solidarity with those in need.

Thirteen: The Kingdom Of God – An Ideal

"Do not worry about your life, what you will eat or what you will drink, or about your body, what you will wear. But strive first for the kingdom of God and his righteousness, and all these things will be given to you as well." - Matthew 6:25, 33

There are consequences to being made in the image of God. We are led to respect the uniqueness and individuality of ourselves and of every other human being.

God's love is not meant for the human race corporally, but for each individual in the most unique and personal way imaginable. Every human being is individually beloved by God.

Christianity speaks of the Church as "The Bride of Christ." This is an important concept, but it is not the same idea. Christ's love for his Church as a whole is something entirely different from his love for each person within that Church.

All being made in God's image hardly means that we all look the same. Rather, it enhances our personal uniqueness. While granting us his image, God also granted us with his individual, personal love. Every person both looks like God and looks nothing like any other human who has ever lived. Everyone, created and beloved by God, has a total uniqueness and a profound dignity, both in their souls and in their physical, carnal bodies.

This theology is why Christianity demands so much respect for the physical body, while some religions (Buddhism and Hinduism come immediately to mind) place less importance on the carnal side of our physical experience. Christians could never embrace the concept of reincarnation because it would be incompatible with our belief that we were made in God's image. It would contradict the personal care God has for each of his creations, as well as Jesus' teachings about the urgency of individual salvation.

The uniqueness and dignity of the individual human body is also why "life" issues are so important to Christians. Abortion, euthanasia, the death penalty, warfare, and economic marginalization of the poor are anathema to Christian values because they represent affronts to the image of God. When fully comprehending that God's image is present in every human life, individual life must be taken seriously. No social or political concerns, including thoughts on the supposed "greater good" of society, can make up for the loss of a single human life. Each life bears the fullness of God's image.

JESUS' SOCIAL PROGRAM

Both Christians and non-Christians often misunderstand what Jesus actually implemented when on earth. It was not a religion—that was implemented by his followers. It was not a philosophy—his mere existence and identity established that. What Jesus actually implemented was a social program. He spent his life advocating for the marginalized in society. This social justice has to remain integral to Christian practice, otherwise it misses its purpose.

An immediate objection will be raised by Christians who say that Jesus' purpose on earth was to lead the way to salvation, not to effect social change. A true understanding of social justice eliminates that objection, however. Jesus' social program was his method of leading to salvation. The one cannot be separated from the other. Social justice is love put into action in society. Salvation is the process of coming into a fullness of love in communion with God. God is shown to us through those who with us share his image. Thus, our acts of love, both individually and as a society, are the closest ways to experience salvation in the here and now—heaven on earth—or, in Jesus' words, the Kingdom of God.

Jesus' social program was built on respect and dignity. This program follows directly from our place as made in the image of God, with the personal uniqueness that comes from it. Maintaining the equality and dignity of every human individual is a necessary consequence of the belief that we are made in God's image.

The poor maintained a constant role in Jesus' teaching because they are often the ones from whom respect and dignity are held. But poverty itself was not something Jesus ever envisioned eliminating. He himself lived a life of poverty and suffering. He said *"the poor will always be with you."* (Mark 14:7) Jesus did not advocate for a utopia, but rather for the respect throughout the human family that would work toward the dignity of all.

It was not only the poor that got Jesus' attention. He championed anybody who was subjected to inequality. In a society that reserved spiritual education for Jewish men, Jesus gave an integral role to women and foreigners. Likewise, he included known sinners like prostitutes and tax collectors in his circle. These examples were not merely theological statements, but rather strong social statements. They were scandalous and revolutionary. Were Jesus here in the same form in our time, I have a feeling his social statements, evidenced by those he gathered around himself, would seem scandalous to today's Church leadership as well!

The social program implemented by Jesus gave tangibility to the theology of a loving God. Jesus never claimed to have a solution for poverty, oppression, suffering, or any other form of inequality. He did not work for political change, but challenged the hierarchy of his time to accept and welcome those who had been pushed to the social margins. He charged his followers to be aware of the needs of the poor and victimized and to help balance the social order through individual acts of love and mercy.

The Kingdom of God is the ideal for society, where love trumps selfishness and elitism at every level, from the individual to the highest rungs of government. Thus Christian social justice teaching does not refer to a specific set of issues, but calls us to live with love at a societal level. Springing from the belief that human beings are made in the image of God comes the necessity to protect the individuality and dignity of every human person. There may be disagreements on how best to effect this justice, but the social goal of all Christians must be the same. The goal is the Kingdom of God, an ideal of love put into action at every level of society.

Jesus' social program and his salvation plan are not separate things. They are certainly not two separate ways of interpreting his purpose. His social program *was* his salvation plan and *vice versa*. He told it to the rich young man in Mark chapter 10. He illustrated it in the parable of the rich man and Lazarus in Luke chapter 16. And he told his disciples plainly in John 13:34: *"I give you a new commandment, that you love one another. Just as I have loved you, you also should love one another."*

THE DIGNITY OF EACH INDIVIDUAL

The world seems very different now from when Jesus entered human history over two thousand years ago, but the urgency of social justice is as great as ever. The dignity of the human individual remains gravely at risk.

All too often, rather than working for the good of our society in a spirit of compassionate love, we end up in political and sociological arguments about how best to fix this or that issue, or which problem should be solved at the expense of another. Arguing about an issue where social justice and human dignity are at stake is always a losing game.

The reality of most hot-button political issues of any era is that the arguments lead us on an ideological downward spiral. Take "life" issues as an example. So much is always made of abortion, but within true Catholic teaching, "life issues" also includes care for the poor and elderly, taking assault weapons out of the hands of common citizens, world peace and environmental sustainability. Yet there are differences of opinion on how best to protect the dignity of human life. Both Conservatives and Liberals have drawn lines in the sand surrounding these issues, using phrases like "non-negotiable" or calling opposition proposals "non-starters." What they really mean is that they refuse to let their compromise sink lower than their designated limit. What both sides fail to realize is that the common ground is not found in compromising one's values, but in reaching for an ideal!

The *ideal* is something far different than a poor compromise. Reaching for the ideal is an exercise whereby we acknowledge our status as "made in the image of God" and behave accordingly. The consequences of doing so are far-reaching.

Jesus never promised a society free from suffering or injustice. But he also said to *"be perfect, as your heavenly father is perfect."* (Matt. 5:48) What did he mean by this, and why demand perfection when he knew it was not humanly possible?

Jesus proposed an *ideal* for society, which is the Kingdom of God. Jesus wants us to use our energy to reach toward personal perfection and a social ideal with every ounce of our strength and intellect.

Father Ugo Nacciarone, a New York Jesuit and former missionary to Africa, said: "To lower the ideal is to imply that human nature is not really made in the image of God."[44] This brilliant statement charges us to maintain our efforts toward social justice. At the same time, it reminds us of true human nature—what it means to be made in God's image.

What would the ideal look like in our society? The ideal would involve a world where abortion is no longer a legislative issue because society has progressed to eliminate its perceived need. It is a world where the poor and elderly are cared for because of a genuine

---

[44] Father Ugo Nacciarone, SJ: Sermon at St. Ignatius Loyola, New York City, Nov. 2012

desire in our citizenship. It is a world where we do not have to legislate gun laws, because society's violence has been healed. It is a world that strives for peace instead of clamoring for war. Finally, it is a world that works for the good and sustainable life of the world as a whole.

Is this the description of an unrealistic utopia? Of course it is. So is the Christian belief in heaven! We will never achieve the perfect Kingdom of God on earth, but that is no reason to settle for less. If we can visualize a better world, then we can work toward it. And if we, as a society, can work toward it, we may be surprised how much closer we get.

Pope John Paul II identifies the ideal, what Jesus described as the Kingdom of Heaven, as all-inspiring love. "The kingdom aims at transforming human relationships; it grows gradually as people slowly learn to love, forgive and serve one another. Jesus sums up the whole law, focusing it on the commandment of love... Building the kingdom means working for liberation from evil in all its forms. In a word, the kingdom of God is the manifestation and the realization of God's plan of salvation in all its fullness."[45]

Lord God, give me confidence to tirelessly work for the fulfillment of your kingdom. Let me not get discouraged, knowing all things are possible through faith.

---

[45] Pope John Paul II: *Redemptoris Missio*, 15

MAKE IT MINE!

Applying the lessons from this chapter in my life:

➤ How am I helping or hurting the coming of the Kingdom of God? Have I sacrificed the ideal in exchange for a poor compromise?

➤ Try to visualize what the Kingdom of God would look like in our time. How would it manifest in your specific society and community?

➤ What tangible things can you do to implement God's Kingdom in your circle of contact? How can you inspire others to do the same? Does the dream seem so intangible, now that you have taken tangible action?

Fourteen: The Joy Of Following Christ

"Rejoice in the Lord always; again I will say, Rejoice. Let your gentleness be known to everyone. The Lord is near. Do not worry about anything, but in everything, by prayer and supplication, with thanksgiving, let your requests be made known to God. And the peace of God, which surpasses all understanding, will guard your hearts and your minds in Christ Jesus." - Philippians 4:4-7

The rewards of following Christ are clear, though it is not an easy journey. Being Christian is hard work marked with an acceptance of challenge and ridicule. The world looks at us and wonders. They even call us mad, and who can blame them? But we have a secret they do not understand. The secret is that the Christian heart is filled with a great, bubbling joy.

"Joy, which was the small publicity of the pagan, is the gigantic secret of the Christian."[46] So said G. K. Chesterton, who describes Christianity as the most exciting, joyous adventure the world has ever known!

I find myself laughing when Christianity is described as negative and restrictive. Many Christians even feel this way before they learn true Christianity. This mindset comes from focusing on the so-called "rules" of Christianity—particularly on what Christian law tells us *not* to do. We discussed this at length earlier.

---

[46] G.K. Chesterton: *Orthodoxy*, chap 9

The Church itself often perpetuates this error. Anyone who chooses to become a Christian based on this negative idea is surely a little mad and even a little sadistic! Who would follow a creed based on what *not* to do? There is no sense in that.

The reason for wanting to be a Christian is in what it tells us *to* do: "Rejoice!" Again I will say: "Rejoice!" There is also a promise: We will know joy if we follow Christ.

Christianity is in every way a positive, not a negative, religion.

The rules of Christianity are given as a guide to mark the path to a life of joy. God wants his children to have joy. His invitation is constant, beckoning us to a fullness of delight. There is nothing sorrowful or heavy in his invitation. The only sorrow comes from turning away from this path. That is why the rich young man in the nineteenth chapter of Matthew went away grieving. It was hardly the demands of Christianity that grieved him. Jesus offered him a path of freedom and joy. His grief was in looking at Christ's joy but choosing instead the confines of his present existence.

PERSONAL AUTHORITY—A PRISON

But why is joy a secret of Christianity? We hardly attempt to hide it. St. Paul shouts out his joy like a trumpet blast in all his letters. He did not know this joy until he was blown off his horse and blinded by it! (Acts 9:4) He had to be made helpless—God took everything from him, only to give back so much more. It was precisely the dashing of Paul's authority that allowed him to learn joy. Joy is a secret simply because it is impossible to know the joy of Christianity without beginning the journey. It requires a turn away from the safeness of our individual authority.

Individual authority comes in a variety of forms. It amounts to a certain ease of life we construct around ourselves. Ultimately, it can be anything that gives us perceived power. We cling to it and call it our right.

We sometimes call the power of our authority freedom. The problem with power is that in the fear of losing it, the very power has eliminated the comfort and freedom we sought the power to gain. We tend to think of our individual authority as a blanket of security, when it really is the opposite. What could be less secure than something we have to make and hold ourselves? For if personal strength even momentarily fails, we lose everything.

When authority is entrusted to another, however, personal weakness ceases to terrify. If authority is entrusted to God, then nothing can terrify.

Sometimes the individual authority we so cherish is simply the importance we place on our own ideas—in being so certain that we are *correct* that we block further truth from entering our minds. What terrible pressure we place on ourselves by giving such authority to our own viewpoints! The thing is, maybe we *are* correct. But by clinging to our own authority in our ideas, we prevent God from releasing us into the fullness of his truth. We have to give up our ideas not only regarding what is and is not correct, but also on what correctness itself might mean. It requires the simple trust of taking Christ's hand and relinquishing our individual authority. At that moment, joy is given the space to bloom.

This is precisely what the rich young man in Matthew could not do. In this case, the young man's authority was his possessions. But rather than giving him comfort and security, they had imprisoned him. In modern times, we often value the authority of our own thoughts, resisting the authority of the Christian creed. This imprisons our minds in the same way that the rich young man was shackled to his possessions. He had no freedom to experience joy. Instead he lived in grief.

Individual authority places every one alone on an island, closed off in the prison of individuality. By giving ourselves over to the authority of God, a doorway is opened into a joyous freedom not previously imagined, but it takes that moment of trusting release to get there.

There is a powerful peace in following the authority of a creed trusted not only by millions of people throughout the world, but by scores of generations, marking ages of history. The Catholic Church has endured longer than any empire. From the apostles forward, there is a fluid history of wisdom, confirming Christianity in a genealogy of brilliance. What individual authority can have the hubris to exalt itself against such a long-abiding tradition of wisdom?

And who would want to? The peace of God's authority, marked by his Church's long tradition, is brought to life as joy.

CATHOLIC GUILT

I am not going to lie to anyone and say that Christianity is easy. It is challenging, and we all take missteps along the way. But difficulty does not imply sorrow. Challenge does not necessitate suffering. By focusing on these negatives, we take all the joy out of the Christian life. So while Christianity is indeed difficult, let's not make it any more difficult than it already is.

Among some Catholics there is a pervasive sense of guilt, binding the mind to supposed failures. The very phrase "Catholic Guilt" is a term of pop culture. Even non-Catholics, if they come from old Catholic families, often claim "Catholic Guilt," as a badge—if not of honor, perhaps of pride. This mindset is doubly harmful.

First, it shows the world a completely misguided picture of the Catholic faith. Second, it binds the "Guilty Catholic" to his individual authority precisely as he claims to be following the authority of the Church. In this mindset, the individual is making himself his own judge, placing guilt where God places grace. The placement of guilt is the individual's way of binding himself to his own authority. Joy is kept out by the dark, dull shield of guilt.

It breaks my heart when I hear non-practicing Catholics express reluctance to return to the Church because they feel they haven't been good enough Christians. Are they afraid God has stopped loving them? It would be like saying I don't want to visit my mother because I don't visit my mother enough. It reflects a complete lack of comprehension in unconditional love.

God's grace is not something that is ever measured. God wants a relationship with each of us and will wait for as long as it takes. God is the loving parent whose door is always open. The last thing God wants is for us to feel bound by guilt and conscience. God wants to give us freedom from these constraints. He even points out the way.

Christianity may be difficult. But the way of individual authority is lonelier and has no reward. Jesus' yoke is easy, and his burden is light. (Matt. 11:30) Why are we ashamed to declare such joyous truth? Have we forgotten why we chose to follow Christ? How the world, so dragged down by suffering and selfishness, could use the gentle and joyous burden of Christ! It is our duty and our privilege to bring this joy to a world in need.

RENEWED DAILY IN CHRIST'S LOVE

Our small ideas bind us more and more each day. But God's ideas are so much bigger than anything we could construct on our own. God's authority is not restrictive like human authority. It is a love so big that it seeks and finds every blessing it can give to those who trust in it. It is a bubbling spring of goodness that renews us each day.

Once we relinquish our individual authority and come with Christ, we discover a life of wonder and light. Every day with Christ is a new adventure. Every dawn is a fresh renewal. Every evening is a well-earned rest.

This is certainly not the description of a religion of sorrow... of dutiful adherence to a rulebook in anticipation of a heavenly reward. No, this is a religion of joy, a religion for the here and now, turning an ordinary world into a thrilling adventure! God's blessings are unfathomably abundant. There is no limit to what God will give us if we open ourselves up to allow him in.

Tremendous peace results when we give our authority over to the one who said: *"Do not worry, saying 'what will we eat?' or 'what will we drink?' or 'what will we*

149

wear?'… your heavenly Father knows that you need all these things. But seek first the kingdom of God and his righteousness, and all these things will be given to you as well." (Matt. 6:31-33) God wants to release us from the stress and uncertainty of our individual authority.

There is no greater joy than the loving embrace of a God who *is* love. Ours is a God who loved the world enough to come into it, live with us, and die with us in order to prove his love. In following Christ, we are renewed every day in love. By passing that love on to the world, we fulfill the work of Christ.

A SHOCKING TRUTH

It feels difficult to step out of our own authority into God's, but we are beckoned with the wonderful promise that God's authority is none other than love personified.

"God IS love." This statement is so profound, so beautiful, that it borders on the ridiculous. It is also so simple. In these three words, no room is left for sorrow, dullness, or limits. If really heard and understood, nothing could be more popular or more readily embraced.

These words also leave no room for lethargy. They are dangerous words that propel us into the world with courageous purpose. They are even *offensive* words, for their meaning contains both command and call. Perfect love is never comfortable. It is challenging.

God is love. How wonderful! How shocking!

The *idea* of Christianity has been repeated so many times that we forget how profound and radical it is. After two thousand years, nothing seems new or exciting about Christianity. But what could be more thrilling than the words "God is love?"

150

Though these words are at first beautiful, they are also challenging in that they require evangelism. The knowledge that God is love compels us to share this love. God's love also contains authority. Thus, in a world where individual authority is valued so highly, even love becomes offensive.

At first it seems strange to hear Jesus, after recounting his own miracles, conclude by saying "Blessed is he who takes no offense in me." (Luke 7:23) But this is precisely the result of Jesus' good deeds, as he well knew. In his time, his miracles and works of love were consistently met with offense, as his message still is today. According to Kierkegaard, it is not merely a question of whether or not one believes in Jesus Christ, the physical embodiment of the phrase "God is Love." It is a question of either believing in him or being *offended* by him.[47] The result of non-belief cannot merely be apathy. Jesus left no room for apathy regarding himself.

It is the fear of offending that tempts us to take the meat out of Christianity. Pope Benedict XVI laments that we have become "satisfied with finding out that by all kinds of twists and turns, an interpretation of Christianity can still be found that no longer offends anybody."[48] This is the interpretation the world wants from us, with its acceptance of all creeds—all individual authorities—as equally valid. The problem is, Christianity *does* offend. It is nothing if it is not shocking.

If we conform to the world's wishes, if we water down the stunning truth of God's character, we

---

[47] S. Kierkegaard: *Training in Christianity*, I, e

[48] J. Cardinal Ratzinger: *Introduction to Christianity*, I. I. 3

eliminate both the purpose and the joy from our faith. When Christianity declares: *"This is right. This is wrong. This is truth!"* it is pointing to the same path which Jesus pointed out to the rich young man in Matthew—the path to freedom from his grief.

Everything that may seem unpopular about Christianity is but the secret path to abundant joy. It is the release from the shackles of sorrow. As highly as we value individual authority, it is a crushing weight from which God longs to free us.

A New Commission

Now comes the challenge to Christians in this day.

God wants the entire world to experience the joy that is life with him. *We* are his chosen lights to manifest this joy. By focusing on the difficulties of the Christian life, we do a disservice to God's evangelism. If all Christians could instead embrace the joy of the journey, the world would beg us to share our secret.

There is no need to repeat the gospel over and over to unwilling ears. Our best evangelism will be done by living in joy—by letting God's love shine out through us.

How can we do other than to shout out our joy from the rooftops? Christ's love is a balm of renewal that has no comparison. If only the world could feel it! The peace and joy of relinquishing individual authority and living in God's is something today's world cannot comprehend. But they *will* notice. They *will* wonder. And eventually they will be drawn.

It is ours to invite the world to experience the great joy of following a God so good that he is love itself! Too long has this light been hidden under a bushel basket. (Matt. 5:15) Let's *burn* the bushel basket and shine the true light of Christianity upon the world!

Lord Jesus, give me the courage to take your hand and step out of my own authority into the fullness of your abundant love. May my joy be a light to the world!

MAKE IT MINE!

APPLYING THE LESSONS FROM THIS CHAPTER IN MY LIFE:

➢ Do I truly believe Jesus' promise to those who believe in him? Am I ever a little offended by Jesus' call myself?

➢ Think about ways your individual authority may be preventing you from experiencing the pinnacle of life with Christ. Pray for the serenity to follow Jesus with joyful abandon!

➢ Think about the ways you are shackled to your own authority, whether it is stuff, a routine, your opinions, etc. Make a list if you have to. Then offer those things up to God. Watch what peace will come from the release..